Johan Ludvig Runeberg

Lyrical Songs, Idylls and Epigrams

Johan Ludvig Runeberg
Lyrical Songs, Idylls and Epigrams
ISBN/EAN: 9783744775021

Printed in Europe, USA, Canada, Australia, Japan

Cover: Foto ©Thomas Meinert / pixelio.de

More available books at **www.hansebooks.com**

JOHAN LUDVIG RUNEBERG'S

LYRICAL SONGS,

IDYLLS AND EPIGRAMS.

Cambridge:
PRINTED BY C. J. CLAY, M.A.
AT THE UNIVERSITY PRESS.

JOHAN LUDVIG RUNEBERG'S

LYRICAL SONGS

IDYLLS AND EPIGRAMS

DONE INTO ENGLISH BY

EIRÍKR MAGNÚSSON, M.A.

UNDER-LIBRARIAN OF THE UNIVERSITY LIBRARY, CAMBRIDGE,

AND

E. H. PALMER, M.A.

OF THE MIDDLE TEMPLE, BARRISTER AT LAW, LORD ALMONER'S
PROFESSOR OF ARABIC, AND FELLOW OF SAINT JOHN'S
COLLEGE IN THE UNIVERSITY OF
CAMBRIDGE.

London:

C. KEGAN PAUL & CO. 1, PATERNOSTER SQUARE.

1878

TO

HIS MOST GRACIOUS MAJESTY

OSCAR THE SECOND

KING OF SWEDEN

THIS WORK

BY HIS MAJESTY'S SPECIAL PERMISSION

IS HUMBLY DEDICATED.

SIRE,

THIS translation is, so far as we know, the first attempt to render into English any of the more important poetical works in the Swedish language, with absolute loyalty to both form and substance.

Having spared no efforts to make this version worthy of the original, we have ventured to solicit the honour of dedicating it to YOUR MAJESTY, who holds so distinguished a place among the Singers in Svea's sonorous tongue.

If, as we would humbly venture to hope, our work should find favour with a SOVEREIGN, who extends such an enlightened interest as YOUR MAJESTY to literature, science and art, we should deem that as the most precious reward for our devoted labour.

We have the honour to be

YOUR MAJESTY'S

most obedient humble servants,

EIRÍKR MAGNÚSSON.
E. H. PALMER.

PREFACE.

In this translation of Runeberg's Lyrical Poems we have preserved the technical form of the original, both as to rhythm, metre and rhyme, rendering, with hardly a single exception, line by line and, in general, word by word.

We believe, that the fidelity of the translation will be found to be almost as close as that of a careful prose version. But while keeping to this strict rule of literal accuracy, we have tried not to sacrifice anything of the beauty of the original. How far we have been successful in this, we must leave it to the reader to judge. It is no easy task to combine in any translation close fidelity to form and substance with elegance of language; and the difficulties are much increased, in the present instance, by the great abundance of feminine, or double, rhymes, which these poems contain, and with which we have not tampered in one single instance.

E. M. & E. H. P.

BIOGRAPHICAL NOTICE.

JOHAN LUDVIG RUNEBERG was born at Jacobsstad in Finland on the 5th of February 1804. His family, to judge from the names of his parents, *Lorenz Ulrich* and *Anna Maria Malm*, seems to have been of purely Swedish extraction, though it had, no doubt, for a long time been domiciled in *Finland*. *Lorenz Ulrich Runeberg* was a captain in the Merchant Service; his small means were soon to be heavily taxed by the support of his large family of six children, of whom our poet was the eldest. It was, therefore, doubtless owing to straitened circumstances, that *Johan Ludvig* was, as a young boy, sent away from home to be brought up by an uncle, a tradesman in a small way of business, at *Uleåborg*. Some time afterwards he was sent to school where, being unable to pay for his maintenance, he had to purchase his education by giving instruction to boys in the same school younger than himself. In 1822, at the age of eighteen, he entered the University of *Åbo*, and after five years of studious toil, and struggle with poverty, took his degree of *Candidatus Philosophiae* in the spring of 1827, and proceeded to the degree of *Philosophiae Doctor* in July, the same year. Immediately on quitting the University, Runeberg left the Finnish coastland, the only part of *Finland* with which up to that time he had made himself acquainted, and went to spend three years in the wild uplands of the country, more especially in the " remote and beautiful" parish of *Saarijärvi*, on the large lake of Päijene. During this visit the foundation of Runeberg's future greatness was laid. The majestic scenery of the country, its wild-woods, mountains, and lakes, the struggling existence of the people, their brave and enduring character, their primitive domestic life and pure morality were henceforth to be the fountain from which one of the most national poets that ever lived was to draw his poetical inspirations. These three years were a period of inward development for that distinct poetical type which in unbroken harmony with itself we recognize throughout all Runeberg's works: in the choice of subjects of an original and mostly national type; in classical purity of conception combined with clearness and distinctness of form; and, still further, in language which is always simple, graceful, appropriate and above all melodious. Throughout, therefore, we are struck with a masterly union of antique sobriety and modern romanticism, which gives a stamp of classical delicacy and refinement to all Runeberg's works.— From this statement, however, one poem (not included in this collection) must be excepted, namely *Jealousy's Nights*, in which the author's accustomed classical selfcontrol and healthy realism give way somewhat to unreality and passionate excess. It belongs to the earliest period of his career, and its excessive passionateness, considering the realistic character of Runeberg's poetry generally, may therefore probably be ascribed to youthful fervour set ablaze by some spark of real experiences of life. It must belong to a time anterior even to that very early period in his career, in which he had come to a distinct understanding with himself with regard to his own type and character as a poet; a period that comes within the time of his upland visit. In these early years of his life, he wrote several of his *Lyrical Songs*, as well as the *Idylls* and *Epigrams* and his translations of *Servian Folksongs*, a popular form of poetry, for which he himself avows great admiration, and the strong influence of which is distinctly traceable in his *Idylls* and *Epigrams*. During these years also he occupied himself with one of his greatest epic poems, *The Elk-hunters*, of which we shall speak presently.

In 1830 Runeberg left the wilds of the interior for Helsingfors, the capital of the country, where he was appointed *Amanuensis to the Consistory of the University*, which had been removed to the capital from Åbo, after the conflagration of the latter town in 1827. This same year he wrote a dissertation in Latin, in which he subjected the tragedy *Medea* by *Euripides* and that of the same name by *Seneca* to a comparative criticism. On the strength of this critical dissertation he was appointed *Docent in Roman Literature* at the University. Immediately after this appointment Runeberg published his *Translations* of *Servian Folksongs*, his *Idylls and Epigrams*, and his first collection of *Lyrical Songs*. In reply to the Dedication to Bishop *Franzén* which Runeberg prefixed to the latter work, he received, some time afterwards, from this great and pure poet the following acknowledgement: "When your charming present arrived, I was prevented, by official duties, from bestowing on it a careful study. I had only time to rejoice here and there in the sight of a violet, or the sound of a lark; but even then I learnt, that it was a real poet, who was making his appearance in my former fatherland. Now I have given a more careful study to the poems, and know, that it is a great poet, which Finland is about to produce."—This prophecy of the purehearted *Franzén* had not to wait long for its ample fulfilment.

In 1831 Runeberg married *Fredrika Charlotta*, daughter of Archbishop *Tengström* of *Åbo*, whose high mental endowments and qualities of heart made her a delightful companion and a devoted wife to the poet. In this year he wrote and published his first tragic epos, *The Grave in Perrho*, the subject of which is taken from the war, which terminated in the annexation of Finland to Russia. It may be called the poet's first trial trip into the tragic regions of the history of his country, which he afterwards explored with so much success, and which furnished him with the themes for his most popular work: *The Tales of Ensign Stål.* For the *Grave in Perrho* he was awarded the smaller gold medal of the Swedish Academy in 1831.

In 1832 he became Editor of the *Helsingfors Morgonblad* and continued in that capacity till 1837. In the former year he first published his *Elk-hunters*. It is not only a truly national epic, but the greatest that Finland possesses after the *Kalevala*. Its greatness lies in the admirably perfect and truthful picture which it sets before us of modern domestic life among the peasant population of Finland. The well-to-do tenant farmer's life is drawn and coloured in all its naïve simplicity, sympathetic good nature, honest love and harmless parish politics, and framed, as it were, by the Finlander's *pörte* or wood-cot, its hearth ablaze with a roaring fire of logs of resinous firwood, its sooty walls of timber, its floor covered with hardened mud, and its roof enveloped in perpetual clouds of smoke. The brighter portions of the picture are thrown into relief by the dark shades which the terribly sad experience of the "honest beggar Aron" supplies; he being the type of stalwart manhood succumbing in the prime of its power to the Finnish farmer's most relentless foe, the frosty night of autumn, which so frequently throws, at a single stroke, a whole happy household on the resources of the beggar's staff. Throughout the poem there runs a vividly felt undercurrent of the sprightliest humour. This characteristic of the poem is sustained both by a variety of inimitably naïve discussions on domestic affairs and family tales, in one of which an ancient flintlock plays a prominent and amusing part; as well as by graphic and almost Homeric epithets, applied to the actors themselves. Thus, to cite a few instances, the stirring housewife Anna, who has got a will and temper of her own, is *the manifold-word-knowing Anna*; while her considerate husband, Petrus, recurs perpetually, as the *thoroughly sensible Petrus;* Ontrus, an unkempt Russian travelling huckster, stands forth, unmistakeably, as the *mattedly-brown-bearded Ontrus;* while the description of the *worshipful tenant of Hierpvik,* retiring, after a toast, foaming beer-can in hand, to the

> Uppermost end of the table, where bench joineth bench in an angle,

is really a gem in its way of descriptive humour.— The classical grace of language in which Runeberg has managed to clothe the whole subject is truly marvellous. We notice, in connection with this poem, one striking characteristic, which meets us in all Runeberg's works, and which, in the *Elk-hunters,* is palpably apparent: the simplicity of the plot. He gives us the impression of all through resisting, on principle, all attempts at artificiality in the arrangement of his stories with a view to a sudden and surprising *dénouement.* He will have such a solution only, as shall stand in an absolutely natural relation to a perfectly simple and natural situation. In this respect also Runeberg is truly Homeric.

In 1832, also, appeared a second collection of Runeberg's *Lyrical Songs.* Two years later, 1834, appeared in his paper a piece, called *The Wooer from*

b

the Country, a comic drama which, though it enjoyed considerable popularity and has been repeatedly played on the Finnish stage, the author persistently refused to admit to a place among his collected works. In 1836 appeared *Hanna*, a delightful idyll in hexameters, which describes happy love in happy summer-hours at a tranquil home in the wooded recesses of upper Finland.

In 1837 our poet quitted the capital for *Borgå*, some distance to the east of Helsingfors, at the Gymnasium of which town a *Lectorat* or Readership in Roman literature was conferred upon him. His poetical powers, exercising themselves here in a less wide range of activity, than while he sojourned at Helsingfors, centered now more inwards and manifested themselves in increasing creative strength and solidity of execution. Here appeared in 1841, the Russian tale *Nadeschda*, as well as the Finnish tale *Christmas Eve*, a story of Finnish military life. These were followed by a third issue of his *Lyrical Songs* in 1843 and, in 1844, by his greatest epic poem *King Fjalar*. In the weirdest of metres and rhythms the poet sets forth the unavailing contest of all-victorious *Fjalar* against the weird will of Fate, which the prophet *Dargar*, familiar with the darkness of Night and the forbidding gloom of deep caves, announced in the weirdest of manners to the king, while banqueting with his warriors in his hall at Yule-tide. The prophecy points to the most fearful fatality that can befall a father's son and daughter. At its announcement

> The hall was all hushed; there met
> The gazing eye such sight, as when showers of hail
> Storming have passed, and calm returning
> Chillingly sinketh over a whitened tract.

The man of many triumphs with suppressed agony of heart orders his children, *Hjalmar* and *Gerda*, to be brought to him. After a terrible battle between paternal love and family pride, the king orders his daughter to be cast into the sea; an order, no sooner expressed than fulfilled. On this same Yule-eve there lies, in the shelter of *Vidar's Rock*, near Fjalar's burgh, a viking, *Darg*, who, Fate willing, saves Gerda. Afterwards this viking is overcome by *Morannal*, king of *Morven* in *Erin*, and is saved from his burning vessel, with a female child in his arms, to expire on board Morannal's ship after having implored his mercy for her. *Oihonna*, as Gerda henceforth is called, grows up, at Morannal's court, and becomes far-famed in song and tale for her surpassing beauty, her hunting accomplishments and her highmindedness. Morannal's sons, *Gall, Rurmar* and *Clesamor,* all burn with love for her, but she scorns them, while avowing her sisterly admiration for their several great accomplishments. The latent cause of this indifference for the royal blood of Morven is, that the fame, which in song and tale flies abroad of Hjalmar, has inspired her heart with profound veneration and intensely ideal love for the unseen young hero. Song and rumour have made her familiar with him through the following facts: while yet young, he prayed his father for a viking-ship, that he might emulate by deeds of heroism on the sea the fame of his forefathers. His father, having then vowed perpetual peace for himself and his people, sternly refuses the son's request. On being pressed, however, he yields to the son's urgent prayer, by granting him, what he meant to be an effectual bar to all further importunity: a ship, which had stood on the shore since his first viking cruise:

> Its keel is cracked, grass up in its bottom grows,
> And through its sides the daylight is beaming;
> Up, take it, fly o'er oceans and seek thy name
> 'Mong strange-sounding sounds, forgotten by me!

Hjalmar calls on the now idle warriors of his father to follow him, and off the fast filling craft is swiftly urged over the trackless fields of the sea-king's fame. Fjalar, hearing this, sets off to punish his son. He soon falls in with an escaped vessel of the fleet of the king of the *Perms* (*Bjarmar*, a Russian tribe), whom, on the previous day, Hjalmar had conquered. A fight for revenge soon follows, and Fjalar is at last reduced to a hopeless defence surrounded by his shield-burgh, or body-guard, when up comes Hjalmar, now steering the proud dragon which, the day before, had been commanded by the king of the Perms, renewing the fight with the escaped vessel, and finishing it with the slaughter of the last man on board. Still Fjalar's errand, the chastisement of his son for his disobedience, was not done yet. He therefore ordered Hjalmar to approach. The latter, obeying, cast away his weapons, and knelt before the stern father, whose sword, as he deals with it a heavy blow at Hjalmar's helmeted head, glances impotently off the casque. A furious order from the father next to uncover the head Hjalmar obeys unhesitatingly:

> Defenceless stood he, having no other ward,
> Than open and cheerful calm on his face.

> Yet lo! the old king faltered now. His sword,
> A death-blow aiming, fell on the victim,
> As faint, as if it had gone to rest upon
> The bed of the bright luxuriant locks.

It was Hjalmar's fate, that thus spake through the listless sword; the son was forgiven, and henceforth pursued his path of fame unhindered.—

At last Hjalmar comes to Morven's strand, to woo the far-famed Oihonna with his sword. On the day, that the fate of Morven is decided, Morannal first tells her the tale of her childhood, how she was picked up by Darg from the waves by Vidar's rock, &c.

Victorious Hjalmar now marries Oihonna with the sea-kings' rites. She afterwards tells him her story as she learnt it from Morannal, and Hjalmar comes, soon afterwards, home to his father, telling him his fearful experience. Oihonna's story, he relates, was immediately followed by this episode:

"So she spake. Blanch not, oh, my father,
Her own blood on my sword thou seest.
Morven's maid, Oihonna, my bride on th' ocean,
Was thy daughter, King, was my sister too.

"Die she would, yea die for me. I bring her
Greeting." Silent he grew. His steel,
Like a lightning's flash, in his breast was buried.
On the rock he sank into death's repose.

Fjalar now bows before fate, and kills himself a vanquished believer.—It is no small accomplishment on the part of the poet, to have succeeded in making a subject like this really pure and healthy reading. Fate works the whole; the actors are fatally inspired, by no innate perversity, however, to act Fate's tragedy; yet in the end so as, in a sense, to defeat Fate itself by atoning for involuntary guilt by their blood wilfully shed. In none of Runeberg's other epics are the characters so plastically moulded and executed, the situations so statelily dramatic, or the whole action so compact. Depth of conception, too, as regards the general subject, and mastery of treatment, make this poem perhaps the greatest of its kind that Scandinavia can boast of in modern times. In mood and strain the poem bears distinct traces of the influence of Macpherson's Ossian.

In 1848 appeared the first series (followed in 1860 by a second) of *Ensign Stål's Tales*, which became at once, and have remained ever since, Runeberg's most popular work. It is impossible to describe the deep thrill which these wonderful romances sent through the heart of Swede and Fin alike, when they first appeared, and equally beyond description is the love of Runeberg's patriotic muse which they have kindled and continue daily to kindle throughout the North. We cannot give an idea—an adequate one, at least—of this treasure of song; we will therefore content ourselves with only a few fugitive remarks. In form and spirit they range over a large region of poetic variety; from the drollest humour, as in *Sven Dove*, who could do nothing right at home, grew tired of scolds, and resolved to be a soldier, thinking that it was, perhaps, a less difficult task to fall for king and country than to work for an ever-fault-finding father on his farm; and on whose heroic death his commander, admiring the taste of the bullet that pierced his heart in preference to his head, transmitted his memory to posterity in the epitaph:

> A middling head had he, forsooth,
> His heart, howe'er, was good;

to sublime tragedy, as in *The Cloud's Brother*, whose noble deeds of valour for his people and land are thus admirably apostrophised by his sorrowing maiden:

> More than living unto me was loving,
> More than loving is to die as he died.

The whole is surrounded by a delightful atmosphere of sympathy with the people, under all aspects and in all circumstances of life. Three main currents, are especially noticeable as running through these songs: Finnish patriotism, Finnish highminded and generous valour, and Finnish intense love, which finds its noblest and purest expression in *The Cottage Girl*, who could not endure life after having satisfied herself that he, on whom she had bestowed her heart, was a coward. More, perhaps, than any other event in the history of Finland, these songs have done to fire the patriotism of the Fins, to brace up their power of resistance, and to make them realize their existence as a distinct nationality.

In 1851 the poet saw, for the first and last time in his life, the country, in the language of which he had been singing Finland's life and nature for twenty years—*Sweden*. His reception was exceedingly enthusiastic, and most of all so among the members of the *Swedish Academy*. His peculiar relations to the Academy made this brotherly frankness especially touching. Runeberg had repeatedly passed condemnatory verdicts on works and talents upon which the Academy had deigned to confer its golden honours. Despite his sledge-hammer criticisms, by which he might be said to be periodically at open war with this institution, it had, much to its credit, of its own accord conferred its large gold medal on Runeberg in 1839, and now each member vied with the other in a fraternal reception of the revered antagonist. This visit, "full of pleasure, sympathy, and honour", the Poet afterwards, while remembering it with great delight, used frequently to denote as an act of heaping burning coals upon his head.

In 1853 Runeberg became a member of "The Hymnbook Committee of Finland"; the labours of this body resulted in the publication, in 1857, of *A Draft of a Swedish Hymnbook for the Evangelical Lutheran Congregations of Finland*, a work which was edited by Runeberg, and to which he alone contributed no less than 62 hymns. Though generally little noticed, it is a work of high merit. The deep devotion, the pure, fervid faith and child-like humility, which meets us in these hymns, in harmonious prayer, most simple in language, and most catholic in sentiment, render this Finnish hymnbook one of the best in the North.

In 1864 appeared, besides *Cannot*, which he called *a family picture*, a sweet and simple drama, the last of Runeberg's greater works, *The Kings of Salamis*, a tragedy in five acts, setting forth the struggle between the usurper, *Leiokritos*, and the dispossessed *Eurysakes*, the son of *Ajax* and *Tekmessa*, which terminates in the overthrow of the Pretender. In this work we admire the clearness of the characters, the unity of the dramatic action, the masterly drawn contrast between the nobleminded *Leontes* (Leiocritos' son), and the loathsomely base *Rhaistes*, who eventually become each other's banesmen, the nobly tragic endurance and touching womanliness of Tekmessa, and, last, though not least, the classical dignity of some of the characters in their bearing, and the deliberately measured language in which they give utterance to their feelings. One feels, in reading this tragedy, as if the poet were holding passion down all through with one hand while, with the other, giving to it a stately and graceful embodiment with features only expressive of passive and patient agony, nobly borne.

Soon after this, Runeberg was struck with apoplexy, and remained ever afterwards a confirmed invalid until, on the afternoon of the 6th of May last, he passed away, leaving behind a widow and six sons, one of whom, Walter, is a sculptor of rapidly growing fame, now pursuing his studies at Rome.

Runeberg's greatness as a poet rests objectively on one main foundation: Patriotism. With a rare intensity of love and sympathy he lives himself into the life of his people, and with the keenest eye for nature, he lives himself into the natural phenomena of his country. To his nation are devoted almost all the noblest creations of his genius. Her joys and sorrows, her hopes and fears he has sung as few poets ever have sung the same or similar themes under the same or similar circumstances: a nature, grand of aspect, certainly, but relentlessly chary of cheer and comfort; and life, met in sparse clusters here and there, like oases in a barren desert, about the foreground of a vast region of moors, lakes, morasses and impenetrable wild-woods, itself so uniform that, for the outsider, one feature only seems to be unmistakeably recognizable: a cheerless stolidity. But subjectively he derives his fame, apart from his mighty poetic gifts, from his ethereal purity of sentiment, his vigorous healthiness of feeling, his dignified control of passion, his universal sympathy for all that is noble and righteous, his sound optimist philosophy and his enchanting melody of language. His name will long be cherished with love and admiration in the North, and through many a year to come will his own words on the departed *Bard* be applied to him :—

> But still his song flies over land and wave,
> Each heart still at his noble memory gloweth.

CAMBRIDGE,
St Valentine's Day, 1878.

E. M.

CONTENTS.

	PAGE
To Franzén	1
The Old Man's Return	4
The Noble Victorious	7
The Lark	11
May-song	13
Birds of Passage	15
The Shepherd	17
My Days	22
To a Bird	24
The Spring Morning	27
To a Flower	30
The Bird's Nest by the Highway	32
A Summer Night	34
The Swan	37
The Cottager's Daughter	39
Autumn Evening	42
Consolation	45
Love's Blinding	49
The Girl's Lament	51
To Unrest	52
The Lover	54
To my Sparrow	57
The Burial	59
To Frigga	61
Youth	63
Waiting	66
Journey from Åbo	69
How blest am I	73

CONTENTS.

	PAGE
The Meeting	75
To a Maiden	77
The Convalescent	79
Lullaby for my Heart	81
Memories of Childhood	84
On a Friend's Death	87
On a Sleeping Child	90
On a Child's Grave	91
Life and Death	92
Old Age	94
The Bard	98
To Yearning	101
The Work-girl	103
The Peasant Youth	105
The Rower	107
The Pine-thrush	109
The Young Huntsman	111
The Morning	113
The Kiss	115
Regret	117
That was then	119
The Sailor's Girl	121
Greeting	123
Mind—for then the God appeareth	125
Serenade	127
Dissimulation	128
Butterfly and Rose	130
The Bird-catcher	132
To the Evening Star	134
The Dying Man	136
The Youth	137
To a Rose	138

CONTENTS.

	PAGE
The Belle	139
By a Fountain	141
The Maid of Seventeen	143
The Revenge	145
The Flower's Lot	147
Who hither steered thy way	148
The Bride	150
Regret	151
Spring Ditty	153
To Fortune	154
The Heart's Morning	156
The Doubter	158
The Bride	160
The Sunday Harvest	162
The Old Man	164
The Flower	165
Autumn Song	167
Coming Home	169
My Life	170
Thought	172
The Forsaken	173
Autumn Evening	175
Waiting	176
Memory	177
The Painter	178
The Two	180
The Vain Wish	183
In a Young Girl's Album	184
To the Ladies	185
Idylls and Epigrams (I—LXII)	191—232

CORRECTIONS, &c.

Page 1, line 13, *for* mavis *read* throstle
,, 36, ,, 7, *for* ere *read* e'er
,, 50, ,, 1, *for* sighéd *read* sighed then
,, 69, ,, 8, *for* ware *read* wear
,, 70, ,, 6, *Runsala*, a beautiful island a short distance from Åbo, and a favourite summer resort.
,, 70, ,, 8, *Choræus (Michael)*, of Swedish extraction, born at *Vörå*, in Finland, 1774, ob. 1806; a noted poet and a preacher of great reputation. A spring, called Choræus spring, is found in the centre of the island of Runsala, dedicated to the poet in the Latin words: *Fons Choræi Phœbei perennis.*
,, 70, ,, 13, *for* lake *read* bay
,, 71, ,, 8, *Lemu*, a foreland, a short distance from Åbo, where Baron *Ramsay (Carl Gustav)* met with a hero's death, June 19, 1808.
,, 96, ,, 11, *for* Alps *read* Alps'
,, 189, ,, 11, *for* strawberries *read* raspberries

TO FRANZÉN.

HAST thou then thy cherished voice uplifted
   Midst us for the last,
Thou who, lark-like, with thy song hast drifted
   Forth from Autumn's blast?

Shall that land which saw thy morning's flower,
   Saw thy noon-day's gold,
Not also thy coming evening's hour
   Sunlit, sweet, behold?

Dost forget in Sweden's flowery valleys
   Native woodlands dear,
And for songs of nightingales, the sallies
   Of the mavis here?

M.

TO FRANZÉN.

Since thou went'st from us, full many a chilling
   Winter saw we pass;
But though spring-time came and song-birds trilling,
   Cam'st not thou, alas!

Yet within thy former groves was dreaming
   Night as sweet as aye,
In the tiniest floweret's eye still beaming
   Selfsame dewdrops lay,

As when blissful erst that strand thou soughtest
   Where thy home-stream flows,
Look'dst on midnight's flame, in verses thoughtest,
   Or didst cull a rose.

Say, when spring shall once again appear there,
   And its splendours burst,
Would it not be sweet to shed a tear there,
   Where thou sangest erst?

Aye, though Uhlå's ancient burgh is shattered,
   Though thou should'st but trace
Dreary ruins, o'er thy birthplace scattered,
   O'er thy dwelling-place,

TO FRANZÉN.

It would yet be sweet to go, inquiring
   Where, in days of yore,
Was the hut, and where the Muse inspiring,
   Which its flag-staff bore.

Though in Aura's schools the wild wind shrieketh,
   Come there without let!
Many a memory there from ashes speaketh
   To thy bosom yet!

Come thou back to that land, which embraces,
   Ah, so gladly thee!
Midst our rocks where'er thy landing-place is,
   Flower-strown paths thou'lt see.

As a yearned-for spring-day shall each dwelling
   Thee a greeting send,
Echo hail thee, through the gray hills swelling,
   As thy childhood's friend.

THE OLD MAN'S RETURN.

LIKE birds of passage, after winter's days returning
    To lake-land home and rest,
I come now unto thee, my foster-valley, yearning
    For long-lost childhood's rest.

Full many a sea since then from thy dear strands has torn me,
    And many a chilly year;
Full many a joy since then those far-off lands have borne me,
    And many a bitter tear.

Here am I back once more.—Great Heaven! there stands the dwelling
    Which erst my cradle bore,
The selfsame sound, bay, grove and hilly range up-swelling:
    My world in days of yore.

All as before.—Trees in the selfsame verdant dresses
    With the same crowns are crowned;
The tracts of heaven, and all the woodland's far recesses,
    With well-known songs resound.

There with the crowd of flower-nymphs still the wave is playing,
  As erst, so light and sweet;
And from dim wooded aits I hear the echoes straying
  Glad youthful tones repeat.

All as before.—But my own self no more remaineth,
  Glad valley! as of old;
My passion quenched long since, no flame my cheek retaineth,
  My pulse now beateth cold.

I know not how to prize the charms that thou possessest,
  Thy lavish gifts of yore;
What thou through whispering brooks, or through thy flowers expressest,
  I understand no more.

Dead is mine ear to harp-strings which thy gods are ringing
  From out thy streamlet clear,
No more the elfin hosts all frolicsome and singing
  Upon the meads appear.

I went so rich, so rich from thee, my cottage lowly,
  So full of hopes untold,
And with me feelings, nourished in thy shadows holy,
  That promised days of gold.

The memory of thy wondrous spring-times went beside me,
   And of thy peaceful ways,
And thy good spirits, borne within me, seemed to guide me,
   E'en from my earliest days.

And what have I brought back from yon world wide and dreary?
   A snow-encumbered head,
A heart with sorrow sickened, and with falsehood weary,
   And longing to be dead.

I crave no more of all that once was in my keeping,
   Dear mother! but one thing:
Grant me a grave, where still thy fountain fair is weeping,
   And where thy poplars spring!

So shall I dream on, Mother! to thy calm breast owing
   A faithful shelter then,
And live in every floweret, from mine ashes growing,
   A guiltless life again.

THE NOBLE VICTORIOUS.

FOR the Noble, brethren, shall my lyre be sounded,
    How the Noble conquers, though its steps be bounded,
How it braveth Evil, how it crusheth Powers:
    Teach thou the world, oh, my hallowed song!

Him, who bleedeth, comfort, though no more he hopeth,
Tell the humbled slave that Freedom's blossom opeth;
And to spoilers' hosts, and guards of tyrants' towers,
    Say, the Avenger is coming ere long!

See, in star-decked mantle goes the villain shameless,
With a pomp, begotten out of plunders nameless,
And in silence sitteth Law with terror smitten,
    Trodden in dust, where the mighty one goes.

But he meeteth Virtue, her calm front upraising,
And he sees her eye upon his own eye gazing,
And he standeth vanquished—and, with red shame bitten,
    Earthward his o'erclouded glances he throws.

See yon ancient lion, that destruction breedeth :
Here a herd is scattered, there a victim bleedeth ;
In the conscious pride of lordly strength he swelleth,
    Sure in the measureless wealth of his might.

But he marks the herdsman, who to help them hieth,
And that nobler stamp upon his brow descrieth,
And, with cowered pride, while yet his prey he felleth,
    Flees to the forests to hide in their night.

But with sword for sceptre, and with blood that
                           crowned him,
Sits enthroned the tyrant, rotting equals round him ;
And his law is darkness, his commands enslaving,
    Death and fell Terror his mandates propound.

And their birth ignoring, and their worth forgetting,
At his feet their incense cringing slaves are setting,
And the hireling crowd, around the castle raving,
    Hail him a god with a jubilant sound.

As a King stands Wrong ; in exile Good is quartered ;
Truth is trampled down ; Humanity is bartered ;
And the lofty thoughts become but dwarf-grown
                                    flowers,
    Bowed to the ground 'neath a traitorous hand.

THE NOBLE VICTORIOUS.

Say, when Nature sigheth for her fane disgracèd,
When the holy day is by long night effacèd,
Where is vengeance, brothers, when shall help be ours,
    Bringing its peace to the down-trodden land?

Lo! not crushed by wrong, nor yet by glaves confounded,
Where the Noble rests, with blood and graves surrounded,
And the angel host to heaven's own child down-wendeth,
    Nursing the Sleeper with freedom and light.

But his strength beneath mild hands itself upraiseth,
And his thoughts' small spark in time to full flame blazeth,
And he opes his eye, on *you* his glance he bendeth,
    Tyrants, and Slaves, and Destruction, and Night!

See, then flies his torpor, and his anger gloweth,
From his heart a cry for down-crushed brethren goeth,
And he smites on buckler, in one oath achieving
    Triumphs of light with a disenthralled world.

And with strength and fervour on his way he treadeth,
Robes of beams around him, like the day star, sheddeth,
And at Winter's night, to tyrants' sceptre cleaving,
    Showers of his red-glowing arrows are hurled.

Then the spoiler falleth ; Night is driven off worsted ;
And a flaming dawn o'er land and sea hath bursted,
And the morning glow of that new day-break hailing,
    Clearly ring out holy Liberty's cries.

But the Noble riseth o'er the joyous whirling,
Calmly into cloudless heaven itself unfurling,
And disgraced no longer, nor in fetters wailing,
    Blissful an Earth in its bosom abies.

But a time shall come, when Space's boundless regions,
At the trumpet's sound, collect their starry legions,
Into Evanescence and to Chaos hurling
    Powers, that the glorious Azure did fill.

But, though suns from firm foundations fall asunder,
And, though Earth in one sigh pass away thereunder,
And, though worlds forgotten be but ashes whirling,
    Lives on the Noble victorious still.

THE LARK.

D<small>AY</small> its course was taking
    Higher; while, awaking,
Joy and mirth from winter's trance recovered;
    Spring its garlands stringing,
    Woods with cuckoos ringing,
Round the hut my well-known swallow hovered;
    Skies with music started,
    Little birds true-hearted
Poured in tune their tiny bosoms' fire.

    Heard I all their pleasure,
    Moved in deepest measure
At the lark's sweet lot 'neath circling heaven:
    Warmest, as it seemèd,
    Of her love she dreamèd,
Fond one, of the bliss to short life given;
    Every note she uttered,
    As she cloudward fluttered,
Thus, methought, it rang within mine ear:—

"Happy he, whom never
Cruel fetters sever
From the longed-for realms of boundless ether;
He, whom song upraiseth,
Who on Nature gazeth
In the forms of Spring and Mate together!"
Thus I heard her singing,—
Echoes doubled bringing
O'er and o'er again her song to me.

With the bright sun's motion
Over land and ocean
To one's southern home or northern turning,
In the valley billing,
Then in ether trilling,
Singing earth's sweet bliss and one's own yearning ;—
What a life of pleasure,
Oh, what joys to treasure,
Lark, oh Lark! within thy little breast!

MAY-SONG.

LOVELY May, be welcome
  To our land once more!
Lovely May, be welcome,
  Playmate thou of yore!
Feeling's god-flames fluttering
  Wake up at thy beaming,
Earth and clouds are uttering
  Love with pleasure teeming,
Forth from spring flies sadness,
While through tears laughs gladness,—
Morning's glow from out of trouble's cloud.

Lay the floweret chilling
  Neath the frost and snow:
Autumn's pale ghost, willing
  To its death to go.
Winter,—like fierce legions
  On the land descended,
Which in ravaged regions
  Rule, the battle ended,—

Sat with icy glave there,
  Victor on the grave there,
Drear himself and dark and cold as it.

  Not a beam was spread then
    On our morning more,
  Not a dew-tear shed then
    Northlands evening o'er,
  Till, by swans drawn, May, in
    Wreaths of flow'rets dight here,
  Poured her gold on Day, in
    Purple clad the Night here.
  Winter's sceptre shivered,—
  And, from bonds delivered,
Summoned then the beauteous Flora forth.

  Now from groves to greet thee,
    And from budding rose,
  Gladly up to meet thee
    Many an offering goes;
  In thy praise but rings this
    Rustling hedge of flowers,
  To thine honour sings this
    Purling brook of ours;
  And, with thankful tongue now,
  Thousand birds of song now
Sing, as we: "Be welcome, Lovely May!"

BIRDS OF PASSAGE.

YE, fugitive guests on a far foreign strand,
    When seek ye again your own dear fatherland?
      When flowers coyly peep out
        In father-dale growing,
      And rivulets leap out
        Past alder-trees blowing,
      On lifted wings hither
        The tiny ones hie,
      None shows the way whither
        Through wildering sky;
        Yet surely they fly.

They find it so safely, the long sighed-for North,
Where spring both their food and their shelter holds forth;
      The fountain's breast swelleth,
        Refreshing the weary,
      The waving branch telleth
        Of pleasures so cheery;
      And there the heart dreameth
        'Neath midnight-sun's ray,
      And love scarcely deemeth,
        Mid song and mid play,
        How long was the way.

The fortunate blithe ones, they build amid rest,
'Mong moss-covered pine trees their peaceable nest;
    Though tempest and fray, too,
      And trouble may lower,
    They find not the way to
      The warderless tower.
    Joy needs, to be full there,
      But May-day's bright brand,
    And Night that shall lull there
      With rose-tinted hand
      The tiny wee band.

Thou, fugitive soul on a far foreign strand,
When seek'st thou again thine own dear fatherland?
    When each palm-tree beareth,
      In father-world growing,
    Thy calm faith prepareth
      In joy to be going
    On lifted wings thither,
      As little birds hie,
    None shows the way whither
      Through wildering sky;
      Yet sure dost thou fly.

THE SHEPHERD.

How fair thro' cloudlets swelling
　　The day doth ope,
And filleth field and dwelling
　　With joy and hope!
From grove and woodland regions
　　Glad voices ring,
And all the airy legions
　　God's praises sing.

Clouds purple streaks are sending
　　O'er azure ground,
And earth's fair hues are blending
　　With heaven's around.
The fountain stands thereunder
　　So clear and smiles,
And to her lap each wonder
　　Of heaven beguiles.

Thee, meadow green, I wander
  Once more around,
Where purling brooks meander
  In merry bound;
By yonder stem decaying
  My turf-banks lie,
And goats and lambkins playing
  They thrive thereby.

How sweet, through latticed walling
  Of leafy bowers,
To see morn's dewdrops falling
  Upon the flowers!
At ease I hear each song here,
  The gentle gale
So often brings along here
  From dale to dale.

Here for my sweetheart's coming
  I'm wont to bide;
Here she, her love-songs humming,
  Sat by my side..
Oh, listen lamb! thou hearest
  Her accents blest,
Soon shall I clasp my dearest
  To faithful breast.

THE SHEPHERD.

When first the sunlight gloweth
   O'er mountain height,
Then yonder hill-top sheweth
   My maid in sight.
To me she bringeth over
   A wreath in hand,
Out of the choicest clover
   Upon the strand.

Then, swiftly speeding thither,
   As on the wing,
Her and her lambkins hither
   I shortly bring;
Here, both the same seat sharing,
   We kiss anon,
And woodland doves are staring
   With envy on.

She sings of nature sweetly;
   The valleys heed
My clear pipe, fashioned featly
   Of water-reed.
And waves are stilled in playing
   On lake-shore then,
And strange herds come here straying
   Now and again.

What are not shepherds given?
  What words express
Their guiltless life who live in
  The dale's recess?
We here enjoy our riches
  In quiet way,
And flock and floweret teaches,
  How great are they.

Yea, e'en when North-winds riot
  O'er buried flowers,
No blast disturbs my quiet
  And happy hours.
I seek in wintry weather
  My dwelling low,
And love and peace together
  Within it grow.

Beside the warm hearth seated
  I linger gay,
While stallèd herds are treated
  To leaves and hay.
I sing the song of flowers
  Within my room,
Though summer's gone, and hours
  Of bud and bloom.

The frost may nip my braes, or
   My lowland site,
But not my simple lays, or
   My pure delight.
Though storms outside are yelling,
   It matters not,
If only calm be dwelling
   Within the cot.

But spring returneth, treading
   In winter's rear,
With wind-flower's eye still shedding
   A dewy tear;
My flock to fields surrounding
   I drive out then,
And hear the echoes sounding
   My voice again.

Thee, meadow green, I wander
   Once more around,
Where purling brooks meander
   In merry bound;
By yonder stem decaying
   My turf-banks lie,
And goats and lambkins playing
   They thrive thereby.

MY DAYS.

IN shady dale, wherein the lark's tone waketh,
   I sit beside my girl with rapture glowing;
Whilst at my feet the fountain's billow breaketh,
   By flowerets kissed and breezes gently blowing:
   Never, on any provocation, going
To fight that ghost, which sorrow's title taketh;
   And there is none who knows my hillock lonely,
   Save friendship and my girl and goblet only.

I laugh, she laughs, my dream's sweet partner, making
   Ourselves no feigned or fancied troubles for us;
I sing her name, she sings mine back, till shaking
   The foliage at our rapture thrills before us;
And butterflies, the floweret's kiss forsaking,
   Swarm up, and form a flowery heaven o'er us;
Oh, beauteous world! how nature all resoundeth
Each note of bliss, which in our bosom soundeth.

Why should I raise an inward discord, breaking
  The harmony o'er all creation swaying?
A pure tone only is through all things playing,
And pure should be my echo, too, awaking.
  Thou, gentle girl, my share of joy assaying,
Shalt, while thine ear our unison is taking,
  Be closer clasped in my embrace, and in it
  Turn life to kisses and each fleeting minute.

TO A BIRD.

OH, little bird, hid yonder,
   Mid elmen leaflets, say,
How canst thou e'er be singing,
   And always be so gay?
I hear thy voice each morning,
   I hear it every night,
In sound the selfsame clearness,
   In tone the same delight.

Thy store it is so scanty,
   Thy dwelling is so small,
Yet, looking toward thy cottage,
   Thou singest glad withal.
Thou gatherest in no harvest,
   Thou canst not sow nor till,
Thou knowest not the morrow,
   Yet art contented still.

How are there not full many,
  Who goods and riches hold,
Who own both lands and kingdoms,
  And dwell in halls of gold;
And yet they greet with sighing
  And tear-besprinkled brow
The sun, whose rise thou hailedst
  With songs of praise just now!

How would not man despise it
  Thy humble lot to fill!
And he, the one ungrateful,
  Is less contented still.
To crush thy tender bosom
  Entirely free he is;
And yet thy fate thou praisest,
  While he is cursing his.

Why should he, cold and frowning,
  His eyes to heaven lift?
What can he claim as his, when
  'Tis all the Maker's gift?
When earth's delight is lying
  His very feet before,
Why should he look with pride on
  The slave, and sigh for more?

Nay, sing thou little bird then
  Of joy the whole day long,
And not one note of wailing
  Will I blend with thy song.
Come, build on every summer
  Beside my cottage now,
And teach me night and morning
  To be as blest as thou.

THE SPRING MORNING.

SEE the glorious sun, that treadeth
   Over Eastern billows yonder,
And his gold and purple sheddeth
   O'er the earth that smiles thereunder.
Gloom is scattered, cold departeth,
Nature from her slumber starteth.

Lately borne on light wings over
   From the South, in sprightly measure
Sing the larks, as high they hover,
   Feeling's hope and spring-time's pleasure;
While in numbers earthward sailing
Flights of swans the North are hailing.

Free and wanton waves are tripping
   'Neath the tree-stems clustering thickly;
Squirrels, glad at heart, are skipping
   Towards their moss-roofed chambers quickly.
Far away in deep woods wooing
True and tender doves are cooing.

THE SPRING MORNING.

Soft in morning breezes swaying
   From the ground the green corn peepeth,
Winter's white garb still displaying
   O'er the blades the hare it leapeth.
Sportsmen, hid in bushes ready,
Raise the hammer slow and steady.

By the wood-chill scarce congealéd
   Here a sunken snowdrift gleameth;
There, by silver-birch concealéd,
   Streamlets brawl and primrose beameth;
Into life the brook-nymph bounding
Now her silver chord is sounding.

Beauteous spring, thy car has tarried
   Long, ere Southern strands thou clearedst;
Ere, to hills forgotten carried,
   In our North thou reappearedst.
Yet the South no bosom knoweth,
That, like ours, so grateful gloweth.

Hear our hymns, how loud they call now;
   Hear thou, what it means, our singing;—
That thou comest to us all now,
   Freedom unto captives bringing:
That where polar snows lie driven,
Hearts are yet found to enliven.

THE SPRING MORNING.

Hasten, and for land and water
   Festal garbs fresh-woven make, and
Butterflies from night's dark quarter,
   From the dust their brides awake, and
Drive from minds, with love refilling,
Bygone winter's memories chilling.

TO A FLOWER.

BURST is thy trance then;—no more confined thine eye
Now with such hearty gladness looks towards the sky,
Where crimson morn, whom the welkin light upholdeth,
In breast of purple Nature, his bride, enfoldeth.

All is so hushed in thine home, so quiet yet,
Of rapture die the breezes, as nigh they get,
On golden wings the fluttering treason neareth;
Say, little floweret, how fair the world appeareth.

'Mid sportive Zephyrs as yet thou canst not guess,
'Mid whispering butterflies and morning-dew's caress,
How quickly ceaseth lover's devotion fickle,
How many a sorrowing tear o'er thy cheek shall trickle.

TO A FLOWER.

Oh, wherefore gave not He of His power immense
Eternal spring to thy flower-life's innocence?
And wherefore may'st thou not look, beguiled so lightly,
On midday's sun, as on Daylight breaking brightly?

So smile thou, little floweret, so guiltless there,
Soon shalt thou find, how deceitful spring-days were,
And ponder, moved, on that former happy minute,
When to the bud confined thou wert dreaming in it.

THE BIRD'S NEST BY THE HIGHWAY.

LITTLE bird, why by the noises rough
    Of the road didst thou thy hut erect there?
Was thy wood not cool and sweet enough?
    Stood they not, the birches, leaf-bedecked there?
Shone not there the crimson morning's light
E'en as here, with sweetness and delight?

Brooklets' silent silver billows swam
    Through those dales' far, far away recesses;
Here deceit, loud rumbling, on its tram
    Heavy, iron-welded, onward presses.
Calm and quiet was seclusion's lot,
Fright alone, poor bird, pervades this spot.

Why exchange for parks so fragrant there
    This embankment, which the worn way lineth?
Why shouldst thou the harried dust prefer
    To the rich hue which in woodland shineth?
Why, to view the world's tumultuous strife,
Give up thine unnoticed peaceful life?

Seems the day not often long, before
  Night's deep calm within thy hut appeareth?
Does thy heart not flutter o'er and o'er,
  When some rumbling growing louder neareth?
Dost thou not full oft enough in dread
Lift the wing, that o'er thy brood is spread?

Wert thou but in yonder distant wood!
  No disturbance there thy heart would harry;
There no fright would scare thy tender brood,
  E'en though thou at times abroad shouldst tarry;
For to them would nature's quiet there
Be what otherwise thy light wings were.

Bird, oh bird, when shortly comes the day,
  When thy brood its feather-sails extendeth,
Then direct its flight, without delay,
  Towards some region, where no pathway tendeth,
Build, and teach them then to build in rest
There next summer each his little nest.

A SUMMER NIGHT.

HEAVEN, what an evening,—how we fare!
    Seest yon ait's small world of flowerets there?
Nana dear, in greenwood yonder
Birds now sing of th' evening's wonder;
Rest the oars, and let us float on
There to land.
O'er the hills the sun shines merry
Still, the creek's wave rocks our wherry,
Evening's breezes bear our boat on
Towards the strand.
Hear'st thou the whispering alder-trees' tone?
Seest thou the meadows, how green they have grown?
Now for pleasure!—swift time neareth,
Setting bounds to our delight;
Nana, soon Love's hour takes flight,
And, like summer's, disappeareth.

Midst the leaves peeps out the cottage now,
Hasten breezes, thither bear our prow!
Seest the old man, Nana, peering
In the door at how we're steering?
And the pretty maid, behold her
Beckoning there,
With her strawberry basket standing
Laughing there upon the landing,
Towards thee, Nana, fain to hold her
Garden ware.
Darling, thou weepest, how holy, how sweet
Is not the guerdon that true love doth meet!
Sent like some angelic creature,
Now enjoy thine envied lot!
Oh how blessed are we not
Only with our heart and Nature!

What no halls of pride have nurtured yet,
Life's enjoyment, Life's fond hope, is met
Growing without aid, and bloometh,
Whether spring or winter cometh,
Where the country wide and free is—
In the cot.
Seest yon duck before us flying,
With her brood to rushes hieing

Poor and bare? yet blissful she is
In her lot.
Ne'er would that wanderer give of them all
One for a palace though lofty and tall.
Not for gold profusely meted,
Not a thousand halls to have,
Would she ere give up her wave,
Or her home in rushes seated.

Evening's coy and gentle love-star, thou!
Look down kindly on our landing now!
Shout, oh greenwood throng, for pleasure!
Be your song a bridal measure,
Which two faithful hearts uniteth
You before!
O'er the hills the sun is setting,
Western skies are paler getting,
But thy colour, Nana, lighteth
More and more.
Late from our sail to our home may we steer,
Still may the morning-beams find us both here.
Home and friends as nothing deeming
Lean, dear, on thy lover's breast.
In this flowery haven's rest
While away the moments dreaming.

THE SWAN.

FROM cloud with purple-sprinkled rim
    A swan, in calm delight,
Sank down upon the river's brim,
    And sang in June, one night.

Of Northlands' beauty was his song,
    How glad their skies, their air;
How day forgets, the whole night long,
    To go to rest out there;

How shadows there, both rich and deep,
    'Neath birch and alder fall;
How gold-beams o'er each inlet sweep,
    How cool the billows all;

How fair it is, how passing fair,
    To own there one true friend!
How faithfulness is home-bred there,
    And thither longs to wend!

When thus from wave to wave his note,
  His simple praise-song rang,
Swift fawned he on his fond mate's throat,
  And thus, methought, he sang:—

What more? though of thy life's short dream
  No tales the ages bring,
Yet hast thou loved on Northlands' stream,
  And sung songs there in spring!

THE COTTAGER'S DAUGHTER.

MOURN for Kandal's daughter, greenwood bowers!
Like unto your blossoms' gentle hours,
Short also were her hours merry-hearted.
Mourn ye, greenwood bowers! she has departed.

Knoweth gloomy death then no condoning?
Shall then nature, for her fall atoning,
To a power, that harroweth and destroyeth,
Offer all the noblest she enjoyeth?

Can the grave's moss-covered keep feel pleasure
Aught so tender and so fair to treasure?
Kandal's child be loved in death's grim alleys,
As in Lanna's grottoes, Vanhais' valleys?

Oh, thou wert so lovely, maid lamented;
Now no more by thirsty youth frequented
Is thy fountain blue, where but the semblance
Shews of thy regret and thy remembrance.

While the fount was thy resort selected,
Were its sweet banks seldom left neglected;
Oft the herd, allured by hope's vain seeming,
There could while away the whole day dreaming.

Sighs of yearning, notes of joy resounding,
Were at home thy rippling stream surrounding,
And along it, clear as mirror flowing,
Nought was heard but songs and gay flutes blowing.

Listen not, oh, Lanna's hoary rocks, now,
Kandal's daughter tends no more the flocks now,
Vainly mourn your voiceless echoes, started
No more by her tones, for aye departed.

Now 'tis lone o'er Vanhais' pastures yonder,
Through its parks no herds are seen to wander;
Some stray bird, p'raps, chased by hawk, is fluttering
There from tree to tree, his sad cry uttering.

Son of Vanhais, thou all else outvieing
In her love, who now so cold is lying,
Hers, of heretofore, a warm heart only,
Say, where with thy grief thou dwellest lonely?

In the wood thine axe all silent groweth,
For the girl no more devoted goeth
Answering to thy voice, as from the clearing
Thou didst stay thy blows with calls endearing.

High upon the strand thy boat is lying,
E'en as though no more thy calling plying
Thou should'st cast out, yon firth's myriads netting,
And wert every once loved task forgetting.

Oh, amidst the churchyard's willows weeping
Thou encampest, where thy love is sleeping;
And from waning day to kindled morning
Sittest thou beside the grave still mourning.

Mourn for Kandal's daughter, greenwood bowers!
Like unto your blossoms' gentle hours,
Short also were her hours merry-hearted.
Mourn ye, greenwood bowers! she has departed.

AUTUMN EVENING.

WHY sighest thou, so oft repining,
    Oh, weary breast?
In nightly hours, when gentle stars are shining,
Why through the silent darkness breaks thy pining
    In frightened strains expressed?

Dost grieve for days on life's isle waning
    Too speedily?
In memory of a spring art thou complaining?
Dost fear the mild law throughout nature reigning:
    To blossom and to die?

Thou mind'st the bird in bright space singing,—
    He felt no woe.
Through woods the notes of nightingales are ringing,—
Their harmonies, are they from sorrow springing
    For fleeting hours?—Oh, no!

AUTUMN EVENING.

The butterfly midst flowers was flying
    One summer's day;
At eventide none ever heard him sighing,
Though faint he drooped his wing, awearied lying,
    Fate's bidding to obey.

When oak-trees fall 'neath time's storms sweeping,
    And mountains cleave,
Thou fool, wilt thou escape death's arrows leaping?
Upon the grave, wherein the Past is sleeping,
    Dost thou revile thine eve?

Who e'er came down thy lot allaying?
    Who sets thee free
From evanescence, and death's smart dismaying?
The floweret's prayer, fond heart, thou shouldst be praying;
    Her dust should silence thee.

The naked desert's manna sharing,—
    The hour's delight,
Go, wander on, a cloudless forehead bearing,
Thou art a stranger, mayest not cease wayfaring,
    Till on thy Canaan's height.

There, o'er the stars, thou shalt discover
    Thy fitting rest.
Rejoice, that all that change suggests, when over,
Is but a dream, which round thy camp doth hover
    In Time-eternal's breast.

Shrink not in fear from that dim glave then
    In th' angel's hand;
He crusheth fetters only, not the slave then;
Transfigured shalt thou look down on the grave then
    From light's own fatherland.

CONSOLATION.

As I sat out of sight
  In my lone dale, my eye
Saw the stars' hosts on high,
How they moved on in bliss
Over mist, over night,
How they beaming dwelt on
In the vast blue abyss;
Then my rest it was gone,
And my thought it was this:—

How unending, oh Lord,
And how rich is Thy might!
By one sovereign word,
But one signal from Thee,
Like the stars' would my flight
Through the vast regions be,—
Yet I'm sighing here now.

And eternal laws bear
Up for ever Thy sway,
And the crown on Thy brow
Shall not rest for a day
Over gray-growing hair.
And Thyself art as free
As Thy glorious light,
And Thy house, a world bright,
Comprehendeth not Thee,—
And Thy child is a slave.

Yet no pang didst Thou have,
That no sceptres nor gold,
That no triumph nor ray,
Render blissful his lot,
But that trouble and ire,
But that gloom and decay
Are the portion he got
From the burgh of his Sire,—
Yet what wealth doth it hold!

And the seed is mown not,
Which from nought Thou didst wake
On the boundless fields' space;
And the tree doth not rot

CONSOLATION.

Thou in chaos didst place,
Though fresh garbs it doth take.
And Thy world is so wide,
Fair and blissful withal,
Spanned of time nor of tide,
On its day's beaming eye
Shall no evening fall,—
Yet a bubble am I.

Just this power had I :
In Thy pomp to delight,—
But no more, but no more,
Comprehend could I not.
And Thou lurest with might
Towards Thy heaven mine eye,
And my longing is sore,
But I reach to it not.

So I thought—and there stood
Then a rose by my side
In the autumn wind bleak,
And all spilt was its blood,
And its beauty had died,
And all blanched was its cheek.

But a stray breeze, that woke
From the hillock, flew by,
And, in passing along,
O'er the languid one swept:
And the stem of it broke
And it bowed down to die.
And I noted thereon,
How so sweetly it slept,
Though its slumber was long.
And 'twas thus I thought on:—

See, have I any cause
O'er oppression to fret
In Eternity's laws?
Only stranger-like set
In mine earthly seed, I
Shall bloom on in restraint;
The restraint where I won
Is the sweetest restraint,
For some day it shall die,
And I hope and trust on.

LOVE'S BLINDING.

YOUNG as yet Love's god was lying
  In his gentle mother's bosom,
Like a star, that in the evening
In the fountain's lap is seen.
Ether's silver sheen descended
Like a dew upon his forehead,
And an ever-rosy colour
In his cheek had hid itself,
While his lips were smiling, fanned by
Fragrance of Olympian nectar,
And the joy of triumphs dreamt of
Innocently played on them.

Paphos' queen, bereft of pleasure,
Shed a tear in passion's fullness,
In the boy's bright eye reflected
Saw her countenance, and smiled.

"Oh," she sighéd "may there ever,
For a memory of my rapture,
This same image in this same eye
Follow thee throughout the world!"

Who need wonder now that Eros
Hovereth amongst us blinded,
Though his sight no band impedeth
And no shades of darkness hide?
E'en among the desert's thorns he
Seeth but Olympian mansions,
Even in the troll's embraces
But the gentle goddess' form.

THE GIRL'S LAMENT.

HEART, mine heart, oh had I but thee before me,
    Didst thou lie, unruly one, in my hand here,
Oh, then should full quickly my care devoted
    Bring to thee calmness.

As her child a mother, then would I rock thee,
Dandle thee up and down, and gently lull thee,
Till thou ceasedst whining, and calmed forgottest
    Trouble in slumber.

But now dwell'st thou shut in my bosom's prison,
Unapproachably barred to each fond devotion,
Only bared for him who, without ceasing,
    Troubles thy quiet.

TO UNREST.

YES, sweetest unrest, long thou, oh long thou still!
    And by no pleasure, let it be e'er so rich,
And by no brimmed enjoyment soothéd,
    Sigh for a happier joy for ever!

Late thy desire was only a loving look
Of one maid's eyes;—and, now she has given one,
    Step higher, and demand her first sweet
        Heavenly kiss, and strive and languish.

And when on purple lips there shall bloom no more
One single rose, whose nectar thou hast not sipped,
    Then hasten, nought but newer harvests
        Under the full swelling veil to covet.

Yes, gentle unrest, sway thou with double might
Within my veins; and call up, with every new
    Acquired laurel crown, another
        Still more noble looming afar off.

TO UNREST.

Thee may the listless fool choose to barter for
A corpse of bliss, he calls by the name of peace,
   And in his shell of calm and slumber
      Creep like a snail upon Fortune's foreshore.

But I love thee! who is it, if not thou,
Who forced me erst to turn to the open sea,
   And with its billows, with its tempests,
      Jubilant wrestle for life's enjoyments.

Thou shalt go with me, oh, blissful angel, thou
Shalt urge me on to enjoy my life-time's day.
   And when it ends, shalt thou in the grave then
      Rouse me up, once more, from my torpor.

And o'er the sun's high path, and the stars also
Shalt thou go with me, shalt in my heaven still,
   O'er happiness's emptied meadhorn,
      Teach me of lovelier worlds to dream on.

THE LOVER.

SETS the sun, the twilight neareth,
    Cooling dew the meadow cheereth,
Evening sinks on wings of roses
O'er the dales devotedly.
Wounded sore by Cupid's arrow
Selma, in her chamber narrow,
By the window oped reposes
Gazing o'er the lea.

Not a sound of lover nearing,
No fond message in the hearing
Of the tender maiden, proveth
That he cometh lightly on.
Looks she with devoted yearning,
Now to mead and woodland turning,
Nothing, but the shadows, moveth
Fleeting off anon.

THE LOVER.

Tears bedim her sight, with sobbing
Beats her heart, her pulse is throbbing,
Now and then a silent sighing
Softly from her lips doth speed.
Vainly! the reply delayeth,
What she hideth or displayeth,
Only roguish breezes flying
Pay it any heed.

In the wind her hair is blowing,
On her cheek light flames are glowing,
White and bare her shoulders shiver
'Neath the dewdrops' chilly rain.
Skies grow dark, the maiden quaketh,
Showers dash, the wild storm breaketh;
Cruel! shall he never give her
Warm embrace again?

Every breath a hope o'erthroweth,
Now she freezeth, now she gloweth,
Passions' flames upon her preying
Now, and nightly breezes now.
Shading veil aside she flingeth,
Round her waist no girdle clingeth,
Free her bosom's waves are playing :
Youth, oh! where art thou?

But he comes.—Rejoice! for sprightly,
Like a star appearing brightly,
Breaks he through the park's high walls, and
Straight to thee his course he steers.
Stands he by the goal he seeketh,
Key within the keyhole creaketh,
Window shuts, and curtain falls, and
Faint light disappears.

TO MY SPARROW.

I NURSE thee, little sparrow, with such pleasure,
   And as at times I stand
With tears within mine eyes each grain I measure,
   Thou pluckest from my hand.

I love thee, though thy veil of plumes display not
   One smile of beauty shown;
I know thee, though thy little beak betray not
   Thy bosom's inmost tone.

Thy garb is dark as night, and e'en thy tongue, too,
   Is dumb and mute as it;
Thou canst not sparkle, and thou hast no song, too,
   Thou'rt but for friendship fit.

Some call thee ugly, and they wonder therefore
   I set by thee such store;
Thou 'rt tender though and true, what should I care for,
   What should I ask for more?

When other people mock thy simple raiment,
  Thou look'st towards me so bold;
I would not give one plume of thine in payment
  For any pearls or gold.

They praise the siskin's trills, they hail with pleasure
  Canaries' shrilly tone;
I sought a being with a heart to treasure
  And warm against mine own.

For love dwells not in outward gloss, nor traceth
  Its satisfaction there;
Its pleasure is the gratitude it raiseth,
  The bliss it doth confer.

When thou dost gently perch in harmless glee on
  My hand and peck again,
Rewardest thou not then my care, my wee one,
  Art thou not pretty then?

Devotedly will I still seek to cherish
  Thy life's swift spring-time here,
And drop upon thy grave, when thou shalt perish,
  A floweret and a tear.

THE BURIAL.

Now the church's dismal bells are tolling,
    Towards the gate a black-garbed crowd is strolling,
And a youth there, from life's spring-field shorn off,
On the bier is borne off.

In the mould the slumberer sinketh slowly,
Peacefully they round the hillock lowly,
And a simple cross by grief was raised there,
O'er the safe burgh placed there.

Now, when life's last tribute had been paid off,
And the hushed procession thence had made off:
'Gainst an elm-tree, growing up there, stooping
Stayed a maiden drooping.

And she tarried till all had departed;
Towards the grave then—towards the dead she started,
And a lily, which she bore in hand then,
Offered on the sand then.

And devoted, weeping, there she bided,
When the sun behind the hills had glided,
And the pallid star, by night o'erladen,
Rose upon the maiden.

Next day found her, as the day before, there;
But her tear-springs had run out,—no more there
'Gainst the cross, to which her arm was cleaving,
Was the bosom heaving.

TO FRIGGA.

'TWILL not tempt me, thy wealth, Africa's golden flood,
Nor thy pearl have I sought, glittering ocean;!
Frigga's heart only tempts me,
When in tear-bedewed eye betrayed.

Oh, how worthless for me would be a boundless world,
With its suns all of gold, with all its diamond sheen,
To that world which with her I
Rapt enclose in a pent-up breast.

What she borrowed from dust, what she from heaven hath got,
Can I tell any more, than, in our summer's cloud,
What is painted by evening,
Or by flowery morning's hand?

Thought grows dizzy and sight, when in her eye I gaze,
E'en as though I looked down on an unmeasured deep,
Till from trance I am started
By a kiss of her purple mouth.

Where wert thou nourished then? Say, laughing angel, where?
Till thou cam'st down to earth, and to thy rosy home
Gav'st the sweet form of Frigga,
Making lovely my wandering here.

When, sometimes, on the way gloom falls, and thorns shoot forth,
When, sometimes, sighs the soul, racked by its fetters' yoke,
Oh, how sweet is it then to
Hie to the loved one's sweet embrace.

Earth caresseth my foot, sweet as a spring-wind there,
Life's encumbering weight feels like a bubble light,
And the fast swelling pulses
Rock the soul to the gods' sweet rest.

YOUTH.

MIDST the Powers, whose throne the earth up-
                                    beareth,
Transiency alone a sure crown weareth,
Death cannot be overthrown, nor spareth,
    And his sickle rusteth not.

Dost thou, youth, fear the Destroyer's power?
Oh, then learn to feast, while lasts the hour,
Know, eternity of life can flower
    In the twinkling of an eye.

Heaven and Earth are both owned by the minute,
Heaven and Earth can be enjoyed within it,
High, and rich, and vast,—though flown by e'en,—it
    Can in memory tarry still.

But not Thought's might, which a strict law tieth,
Feeling's might the hour dignifieth;
Feeling reapeth, while one moment flieth,
    More than thousand ages sowed.

Youth, rejoice, the gods' good bounty flowers
Still in thy warm pulses' summer-hours;
Still within thine own heart's sacred bowers
    Liveth feeling strong and young.

But they flee, at last in numbness ended,
These short hours that on thy bliss attended,
Old age nears, youth, be thy care expended
    On the gifts of life's young spring.

Take thy pleasure while thy May-day lasteth,
Autumn's storm-stride every flower blasteth,
No devoted sun its mild rays casteth
    Over winter's long chill night.

Wherefore art thou, aimless toil employing,
Pleasures single shortlived day destroying?
Wherefore with thine own fresh heart-blood cloying
    Care's and chance's light caprice?

Love exhorts thee, hear his bidding, early
Calls the young god, crowned with triumphs, clearly,
In thy bride thou clasp'st no maiden merely,
    All the world thou claspest then.

Sways the vine, the grape its red blood sheddeth,
Joy alone through her domain there spreadeth,
Happy as a king the beggar treadeth,
    Brothers, 'neath the vineleaves' crown.

Love then, youth, thy heart's flame's disappearing,
Drink, a winter without grapes is nearing,
Laugh, be glad, thy life with frolic cheering,
    Frost and numbness follow soon.

WAITING.

How long the way is!—short for the cheerful spirit,
But long, ah, long for the sickly heart that waiteth.
When will she come then, when will the darling sink down
    Blest on my quick-throbbing breast?

Here will she come though; yea though she but chose to wear out
On woodland's sand-bestrown path her foot so tender.
Here, though she love the billows, and bold in wherry
    Cleave through the mirrory deep.

From foreland's rock, in shade of the crooked pine-tree,
Will I a far-gazing look by turns let fall on
The pathway now, and now on the glassy
    Strait, and its beaming expanse.

Here will I listen ;—be silent, ye merry songsters,
In greenwood tops there, your singing I desire not.
Nay but a soft report of a far-off oar-stroke,
    Or the belovèd one's steps.

In vain ;—for not one sound of the darling stilleth
My ear's desire, but the trills of finches die in
The country's calm, and sometimes in echo's lap some
    Cuckoo's melodious sigh.

Scanning the wood, I see there a gathering only
Of frightened sheep back to some fold returning,
Scanning the billows, only a crowd of mews there
    Gleam in the evening's glare.

But thou, whose eye bright beaming at once em-
                                      braceth
The planet's triumphant course, the atom's slumber,
Say, ere thou settest, oh, glowing Sun, where is she?
    Say where my darling abides.

In vain! for like a king, from thy high path yonder,
Thou scatterest wealth, but children's sighing hear'st
To me, that beg for only one word about her, not ;
    Givest thou torrents of gold.

Whom shall I question? Is it the gay lark yonder,
Who lately on shortened wings sank down from the
cloudland?
Aye! or the hawk then, where he with sails expanded
   Shoots in aërial chase?

Aye, every pulse increaseth my pain, my longing;
Deluded senses nourish my hope with treason,
And hope again with traitorous lips is fanning
   Love's glowing embers to flame.

Nor cools the evening haze, from the wave arisen,
Nor dew's all-plenteous shower my heart's sore yearning,
Nor nightly wind, which round the rocks now whistling,
   Plays with my chill-smitten locks.

To rest now goeth nature, still more there spreadeth
Yon silent shadow over the earth its cover,
In every floweret swelleth a still small bride-song,
   I only languish alone.

JOURNEY FROM ÅBO.

NOW flaps the sail, the yawl is already off;
  Seizeth the rudder the young man's trusty hand,
And in the bows sits, fair and blooming,
Holding an oar there, a country maiden.

The small unsteady boat is no more born down
By milk and fruit, the pails all empty stand,
And gaud and high-day ware is folded
Down in the well-packed apple-basket.

But evening's breezes freshen up anew,
And Aura's pennants point to the bay again,
The sail now fills, farewell is wafted
Gladly to many a boat in harbour.

And now, oh, town, farewell, and a long farewell!
Soon shall I see no more thy splendours proud,
No more shall hear aught of thy wagons'
Loud rumbling din in the crowded markets.

But wander undisturbed in a nature calm,
Its splendour see unmarred by the hand of man,
And listen blest to the country's tongues there :
Birds, and echoes, and silver brooklets.

Lo, how the bay opes towards us its wide embrace.
In the offing looms the strand there of Runsala.
There, among oaks of centuries' standing,
Nymphs are on guard at Choræus' fountain.

Peace with thy ashes, bard of my fosterland!
Like me, thou oft didst rock on Aura's bay,
And often, often lookedst with longing
Back to thy dale and its green-clad guardians.

But now our course tends eastward—the long, long lake
Stands like an endless mirror before mine eye ;
And, white as swans to look at, cleaveth
Sail upon sail through its glassy surface.

The sun is setting, breezes are dying off,
In woodlands hushed is every song-bird's note ;
But here and there a country maiden
Lifteth her oar up and laughs and singeth.

But lifetime's joyous dream on fair nature's breast,
The heart's sore longing, the modest maiden's pain,
And hope's delight, and memory's pleasure
Soar in the bosom of song round the inlets.

It grows not dark, nor light—but so grandly vaults
A night of silver, instead of a day of gold,
Above the boat, while yet it slowly nears the
Bay, that is cleft by Lemo's foreland.

With joy and sadness see I the regions now,
Where thou, lamented youth, thy first laurels culledst,
Where, Ramsay, thou, round guarded standard
Ralliedst again the flying warriors.

With sadness; when I think thou wert ta'en so young
From hope's all-lovely world from thy warrior life;
With joy, though, when I think that the hero
Bled for his honour and native country.

And still with awe the son of the skerries thinks,
In gloomy nights, he sees thy spectre there,
And, when on the strand the pine-trees whistle,
Hears thy commanding voice exhorting.

Thus 'mid calm memories steers our merry course,
Till Vappar's wide firth is all left behind,
And, with its church, afar off the Sound there
Bids us come to its narrow bosom.

There, on the hills, I see the green birches now.—
I greet you, silent witnesses of my bliss;
And thee, oh hut, on the strand erected,
Rented for me for the fleeting summer.

Receive me now, and let me one winged hour
'Mid sleep and dreaming dwell in thy calm embrace;
When glows the earliest beam of morning,
Waits for me Frigga on the hill already.

HOW BLEST AM I!

HOW blest am I!—In lifetime's morning hour
    Around hope's gleaming seas I sweep away,
E'en as the sailor in the yawl doth scour
    The mirrory creek upon a summer's day;
Where'er he looks, a leaf-decked hillock shimmers,
    A glittering scene of flowers his glances trace,
And beaming heaven's high vault o'er him glimmers,
    And beaming laughs beneath the water's face.

How blest am I!—Stand not the earth's broad lands here
    A boundless path for me to walk along?
Have I not ample treasures in my hands here,
    My lyre attunèd, and my merry song?
Have I not speech, that to the heart appealeth,
    E'en though 'mongst Afric's naked sons I move:
The fresh repose, that brightened brow revealeth,
    And in the freeborn eye the look of love?

How blest am I!—In myriad aspects dancing
   The fair Ideal round my path I see,
And at its end there Honour stands, advancing
   Her wreaths, and laughing calls and beckons me.
And Immortality's calm sun sheds gold on
   The goal I seek with yearning's ardent zest,
And not a low, unworthy doubt takes hold on
   My dauntless, haughty, youth-refreshèd breast.

How blessed am I!—A faithful maiden shareth
   My tenderness, my memory, and my hopes.
And if one missing joy my bliss impaireth,
   I seek it straightway in the arms she opes.
Before her glances innocently warming,
   In glorious flowers my feelings' spring doth start,
And butterfly-like come her kisses swarming
   Around the Eden that pervades my heart.

How blest am I!—When life-time's morning paleth,
   My lyre remains to comfort me again.
How blest am I! When e'en my lyre, too, faileth,
   A name, instead, may yield me comfort then.
And if the tongue of fame forgotten leave me,
   My gentle maid will still with me remain;
And e'en should fortune of her sight bereave me,
   The memory of my past shall I retain.

THE MEETING.

BESIDE the hazel-hedge's gate
   She stood, the girl I love the best;
Her glance, that roved so free of late,
   Did now in silent sadness rest
Upon the mound, where, yestere'en,
So happy by my side she'd been.

A tear-besprinkled rose she bore,
   A keepsake which I gave her there;
She thought me on some far-off shore,
   Yet we so near each other were;
Hid in the next bush was I lain,
And weeping looked, and looked again.

There stood a birch from long ago,
   And green and stately had it grown,
It bore my maiden's name,—also
   Bore on its shining bark mine own;
Each by the other I had scratched
One evening as alone I watched.

So dearly it her fancy took
   To see them daily in their place,—
But now she stood and sighed to look
   Upon her loved one's well-known trace,
And wrote a mournful couplet there
From "Ingborg's Plaint" out of Tegnér.

But I kept silence, hiding on,
   And let my maiden's sorrow be;
It was so sweet to think upon
   The pangs the darling felt for me;
For this alone ungrateful I
Did not that instant forward hie.

To flowerbuds flew the butterfly,
   And flowerets gave their lips so red;
The thrush he sang in birches high,
   And straight his mate towards him sped;
Then called I on my maiden too,
Sprang up, and to her bosom flew.

TO A MAIDEN.

MAIDEN, say, what is the magic rare
  Drives me to thy heart with such persistence?
Tell me, wherefore am I longing there,—
  Only there to dream away existence?

Wherefore is that beauteous, sacred spot,
  Wherein nature is as priestess staying,
Stark and joyless to my eye, when not
  Thee among its wonders, too, displaying?

One like me, into dust's fetters hurled,
  One like me, a prey to fortune stormy,
Thou for me art more than all the world,
  Though the smallest bush can hide thee for me.

Darling, long ere I had looked on thee
  Was I loved, and love with love returnèd;
O'er the clouds was then the home for me,
  There had I a cherished partner earnèd.

Richer far her bosom was than thine,
   And her kiss had fuller joy within it;
Wide as heaven was her breast, yet mine
   Not too narrow to embrace her in it.

Oh, how I review them o'er and o'er,
   Memories of my father's house recallèd;
What I loved, when I was free of yore,
   Love I still, although in dust enthrallèd.

Maiden, not thy figure's charms diverse,
   Not the hue thy rosy cheek containeth,
No; a love for all the Universe
   Is the power, which to thy bosom chaineth.

Earth and heaven, which I possess in thee,
   But in thee can to my breast be strainèd,
Wonder not then, that thou art for me
   Dear, aye dear, as if I both had gainèd.

THE CONVALESCENT.

OH, let me sit silent on thy bed and notice
    How spring doth gently sprout out of winter's
                                            torpor,
And, decked in purple, and wreathed again in flowers,
    Promiseth joyfuller days.

I sat, not long ago, by thy side, oh, maiden,
Thy hue was wasted then, and thine eye o'er-clouded,
And death's wan pallor lay as a dreary snowdrift
    Over thy countenance spread.

Now he hath fled, and laughing again there beameth
On me thy charming look, like a brightened May sun;
And in the sweet cheeks' glowing warmth are swelling
    Roses and lilies again.

And every mirth, and all the sweet little graces,
That frightened fled from under the Chill one's sceptre,
Assemble again, now round thy brightened forehead,
    Now round thy ruddy ripe mouth.

Their graceful frolic will I behold a moment,
How butterfly-like they hail each new-born beauty,
Till with a butterfly's courage myself I sink down
    Lively, to frolic with them.

For every tear I shed on thy winter, maiden,
Shall then thy spring return me a pretty flower;
For every sigh thy pallid lip hath cost me,
    Gives me the fresh one a kiss.

LULLABY FOR MY HEART.

SLEEP, oh heart so unruly, sleep!
   Heed not worldly things loved or loathed!
  Ne'er a hope thy peace disorder,
    Ne'er a vision thy quiet.

Wherefore lookest thou still towards day?
What expectest thou more of it?
  For thy deep-pierced wound, it may be,
    Some restorative flower?

Wretched heart, now thine eyelid close,
Day-time's roses thou'st tried enough,
  Only slumber's gloomy garden
    Bears the stem that shall heal thee.
  M.

LULLABY FOR MY HEART.

Sleep, as the lily that slumbers off,
Crushed in autumn by fleeting winds;
  As the hart, weighed down by arrows,
    Droppeth to sleep and bleedeth.

Wherefore sorrow for by-gone days?
Why remember how blest thou wert?
  Sometime spring must fade and wither,
    Sometime, oh heart! thy gladness.

Even thou hast thy May-day seen,
What, if it cannot last for aye!
  Only seek its gentle fires not
    Still 'midst shadows of winter.

Mind'st thou the hours of bliss e'en now?
Groves were verdant and song-birds sang,
  And thy love-abounding temple
    Was the odorous hillock.

Mind'st the bosom that clasped thee there?
Mind'st the heart that sought for thee?
  Mind'st thou yet the kiss-o'ercovered
    Lips with languishing oaths then?

Then, when eye into eye did look,
Feeling mirrored in feeling lay,
  Then was the time, oh heart! to waken,
    Now to forget and slumber.

Sleep, oh heart so unruly, sleep!
Heed no worldly things loved or loathed,
  Ne'er a hope thy peace disorder,
    Ne'er a vision thy quiet.

MEMORIES OF CHILDHOOD.

I MIND a time, I mind it every hour,
   When life's young May upon my cheek was glowing,
And in my tender breast a rose in flower
   With beauty yet unmarred by storm was growing.

How blest then in my innocence lived I,
   Like morning's early breeze through valleys playing:
My joy was pure as daylight in the sky,
   My cares as light as pearly dewdrops weighing.

Then gladness seemed on every form to fall,
   Earth smiled as though by angel hands supported,
The whispering wind, the brooklet's song, and all
   Were babes, as I was, and with nature sported.

But soon thou fleddest, childhood's springtime dear,
   No more to warm this heart again, ah, never!
Ah! woodland's beauty buds from year to year,
   But lifetime's blossom only once for ever.

In vain, when once there weareth off the bloom,
   Its root the water of your tear-flood drinketh;
The whitening leaflets seek but for a tomb,
   The stem against its chilly mother sinketh.

But all too soon these hours do pass away,
   Which here on striving and on hope one spendeth;
Why, when so short man's path was meted, say,
   Should fade its joys, ere yet the course he endeth.

On thee I gaze, oh time, for ever flown,
   A sailor o'er the dwindling sea-coast sighing,
To laugh and play was childhood's lot alone,
   And youth's is one of strife and self-denying.

What is the world, doth to my hope unfold,—
   The palm my bold foreboding sets before me?
What to the hut, where I grew up of old,
   The wreaths, the valley of my childhood bore me?

Yet I repine not, joy that is no more,
   The heart's dove-messenger retrieveth never;
But memory sweet of bygone days of yore,
   Be thou my trusty follower for ever.

Mayhap some friend, the journey o'er, will then
    The bowed-down wanderer pity, tenderhearted;
Perhaps, that old age yet may give again
    My former peace, my childhood's dreams departed.

When on my staff in feeble hand I shrink,
    And see the room where sorrows ne'er betide me,
I'll totter gladly to the deep grave's brink,
    As many an eve erst towards my cot I hied me.

ON A FRIEND'S DEATH.

TOO transient then was the happiness
    That stunned me;
Like spring-day's breezes, with one caress
    It shunned me.
While sweetly dreaming,
Self nothing deeming,
Came he who hid all my joy so beaming
    The grave in.

How fondly, tenderly, name I thee,
    No more now;—
Thou hear'st me not, nor dost ope to me
    Thy door now.
No tears discover,
No sighs recover,
The breast that ashes and night now cover
    The grave in.

Yet I, sweet friend, though by Fate's hard blow
    Oppresséd,
My grief count sweet, and my wound also
    As blesséd;
For thus thou gainedst,
To peace attainedst,
The calm I missed thou two-fold obtainedst
    The grave in.

Blest thou, with thy staff laid down, asleep
    Now lying;
On earth its bliss doth the heart first reap
    In dying.
To fate, disquiet,
To storm and riot,
How deep the peace and how calm the quiet
    The grave in!

Sleep, happy spirit, where guile no more
    Nor bale is;
Sleep light as dew which at eve spilt o'er
    The dale is.
Till dawn's hour gleameth,
Through heaven beameth,
The slumb'rer from morning sleep redeemeth
    The grave in.

ON A FRIEND'S DEATH.

The seed of life, hid in all mankind
    By light here,
No bonds of dust shall for ever bind
    In night here.
What death down-bringeth,
That he up-bringeth,
And but a bud, whence the floweret springeth,
    The grave is.

ON A SLEEPING CHILD.

HOW blest in cradle's lap thou restest there,
   How unaware of error and temptation!
Thy bed—a mother's hand it did prepare,
   Thy rest—thy kinsfolk from a higher station.

As 'neath a morning's calm the still blue spring,
   Thy lifetime's guiltless wave in peace is sleeping;
For Time hath not yet struck it with his wing,
   Nor Fate gone o'er it yet in storm-blasts sweeping.

Thou smil'st,—oh, were there but revealed to me
   The image in thy closed-up eye now playing!
'Tis not yet earth, that thus enchanteth thee,
   It is a memory from far heaven straying.

Sleep, tiny babe! how sweet thy lot to-day,
   To join thy heart's life to that of a flower,
Within thy looks let sleep alone hold sway,
   Dreams angel only in thy breast have power.

ON A CHILD'S GRAVE.

WHO measured out thy struggle, say,
    Young child, now gone to sleep, away
From all earth's grief and gladness?
Thou didst but see its springtime here,
Yet in thy looks but dwelt the tear,
    Within thine heart sore sadness.
Now is thy calm restored to thee,
Now sleep'st thou deep and blissfully,
As 'neath the storm and shower
Doth rest the fallen flower.

That lot is sweet, that victory fair,
To fall at morn, and yet to share
    The day's full wages for it.
Ah, many walked in sorrow's dale,
And saw its dawn oppressed with bale—
    Saw, peaceless, eve fall o'er it;
But came not, as thou, to their goal
With purified and spotless soul,
When Heaven from sorrow bade them,
To where the palms should shade them.

LIFE AND DEATH.

LIFE'S fair angel sat upon the Maker's right,
  In her childhood still the Earth reposed below;
And the Highest looked in anger from his height
  On the first sin, that already there did grow.

Fly, so did God say unto life's Angel then,
  Bearing punishment to Earth's guilt-covered dale!
Not a joy shall bloom for ever there again,
  Not a being 'scape from evanescence' bale!

And God's envoy flew down to the sinful land;
  At his Lord's behest the scythe swang from its sheath.
Saw the son of dust the traces of his hand,
  And, affrighted, named the luminous angel Death.

And the mighty Reaper spareth not, his glave
   Crusheth seedlings slight, and stately oaks doth smite,
High and low, and rich and poor, and king and slave,
   All before his sternness quake, before his might.

But out of the victims whom he felleth there,
   Gathers he, what noble hid in them had lain;
Sifts it but from dust's contagion, to transfer
   All atoned unto its God, its home again.

OLD AGE.

ON the past art thou thy grief expending,
   Grand old man, reserved and silent wending
  Slow thy way through chill old age's plain?
On the hours dost thou regretful ponder,
When thou nursed'st each feeling's wealthy wonder,
And the youthful, fervid pulse was swelling,
   Now with blissfulness and now with pain?

No delight upon thy road is growing,
Love's and honour's standards bravely flowing
  Far from thy deserted pathway soar;
And content's sweet breezes balsam-laden,
Goblets' nectar and the rosy maiden,
Quicken weaklings, quicken slaves oppresséd,
  Ah, but quicken thine own self no more.

OLD AGE.

Are thy pains and struggles then redresséd
By those limbs with Time's deep stamp impresséd,
   This desire, that ne'er its goal attained?
Can there in thy wasted form be tracéd
Any joy or wealth, which has replacéd
Gladness, that with spring made its appearance,
   And, a mere delusion, with it waned?

Yes, within thine inmost deep were wakéd
For each yearning, which by Time was slakéd,
   Higher joys, desires of purer aim.
But thine outer veil do we discover,
But the furrows, which thy forehead cover,
Not the angel Peace within thy bosom,
   Not the Eden which he there did frame.

See, while daytime's purple flames are gleaming,
Charms us now a haze in gold-rays beaming,
   Now a flower, that from its bud hath blown.
When the sun's mild flames are first retiring,
Flies the dazzle which the dust was firing,
And in beauty all untransient glitters
   Then the firmament all star-bestrown.

So when long eve of old age is falling,
Fly the soul's terrestrial troubles galling,
   And its heaven in radiant glory opes.
Is it so hard to forsake life's day then?
Canst thou wish again its splendours gay then,
With thine eve bright as yon starry region,
   And, unlimited as it, thy hopes?

All that erewhile as the sweetest caught thee,
All that strife and fortune ever brought thee
   Stands a faded nothing for thy sight.
As for him, who o'er Alps mountains paces,
Lie the dale's balm, butterflies and graces,
When the mountain's free top he attains, and
   O'er the clouds is cooled in ether bright.

Oh, what is the bliss here prized so dearly?
But a flower-decked troll, a goblin merely,
   Which our fancies from its night unfold.
Yearning stretch we out our hands to grasp it,
Jubilant sink on its lap to clasp it,
But, like smoke, the phantom wraps around us,
   Peaceless, gloomy, tantalizing, cold.

OLD AGE.

Happy thou, whom guile no more betrayeth,
Every lie, that earth's false spring displayeth,
   Hast thou learnt to keep with scorn at bay;
All change from thy safe camp thou repressest,
What thou seekest, hopest, and possessest,
Is not in mortality's parks fostered,
   Shall not with their splendours fade away.

Safe from passion and from vice confounding,
With a memory sweet as harp-tones sounding,
   And a grave that smilingly allures,
And beyond the grave a voice controlling,
Calling, bidding, soothing, and consoling.
Such the bliss for which thy longing aimeth,
   And old age's tranquil path secures.

Hail thee, who away from storms and years now
High, triumphant in thy silver hairs, now
   Wanderest towards eternity's near strand.
Like the sailor, rocked at last in quiet,
   Looking on the distant ocean's riot,
Who with joy's white streaming pennant haileth
   Fain the coasts upon his fatherland.

THE BARD.

WITHIN the dale his young life passed away,
    Calm as the brook that by his cottage bubbled,
In hope and peace came rich each new-born day,
    Nor by the fled one was his spirit troubled.

Himself he dreamt not of his future yet,
    And none divined of coming years his duty;
His world was small, yet greatness there was met,
    And even spring could there awake its beauty.

Shut in himself, and unobserved withal,
    Conversed he with titanic nature, learning
The words of might from rushing waterfall,
    From brooks and woods the tender words of yearning.

There saw he rocks in safety storms defy,
    An image of brave men and heroes showing;
There woman's soul shone through the azure sky,
    And love burst forth in flowers o'er meadows growing.

Thus was he reared, and large became his mind,
  His breast acquainted both with pain and pleasure;
Then took he leave of hut and mother kind,
  Left childhood's valley with his lyre for treasure.

And through the world he wandered with his song,
  To every castle, every cot invited;
He sang—and slaves forgot their chains and wrong,
  And at his strains kings' brows with joy were lighted.

When high he stood forth in a burg of fame,
  Some mighty deed in minstrelsy reciting,
Then beamed the lord's eye like a starry flame,
  While knights stood round the throne their bucklers
    smiting.

The damsel listening to him sat at rest,
  Her eyes around the proud assembly hovered,
And while all crimson grew her cheek, her breast
  Was stormed by feelings till then undiscovered.

So sang, so spent he his life's springtime fair,
  And so his lifetime's beauteous summer hours,
Till time at length brought winter to his hair,
  And 'neath it old age blanched his fresh cheek's
    flowers.

Then back again unto his home he hied,
  And took his harp once more to tune to stir it;
And smote a deep accord on it—and died,
  And gave to spirits' fosterland his spirit.

The stone now crumbleth on the minstrel's grave,
  Which, where for ages lay his dust, now showeth;
But still his song flies over land and wave,
  Each heart still at his noble memory gloweth.

TO YEARNING.

TO Gods of earth my song hath not arisen,
  My lyre's own voice as offering I impart
To Yearning, to the mourner in the prison,
  Unknown and hidden nurtured in my heart.

There, 'midst life's sorrows, is the High one dwelling,
  With memories dim from past times in his breast,
And tears within his gloomy eyes are swelling,
  And by his out-stretched arms but void is pressed.

Oh, wherefore can I not his days delight now,
  Nor find some cool to slake his bosom's brand!
What wings would bear me to the source of light now,
  And give the stranger there a fatherland?

Eternity's vast wealth alone atoneth
  The proud one's wishes' agonizing flame;
And as a king the rigid crown he owneth,
  The angel here scorns joys of every name.

And therefore he, each time the dawn is breaking,
    With tears looks up towards the hateful days,
And therefore measures every breath I'm taking,
    And gloomy counts each beat the heart betrays.

Have patience, guest from higher stations hailing!
    Though hard, thy time of trial is not long;
A night shall come, thy watch in slumber veiling,
    And free thee gently from thy fetters strong.

Thyself released shalt soon on wings ascending
    From earth to a transfigured haven fly;
Thy way o'er stars, and over matter wending,
    Thy heaven reach, thy fatherland on high.

THE WORK-GIRL.

OH, if, with church bells ringing clear,
   I did but stand in feast-day gear,
And saw the night and darkness fly,
And Sunday's lovely dawn draw nigh!

For then my weekly toil were past,
To matins I might go at last,
And meet him by the churchyard, too,
Who missed his friend the whole week through.

There long beforehand does he bide
Alone upon the church-bank's side,
And scans across the marshes long
The sledges' and the people's throng.

And she, for whom he looks, am I,
The crowds increase, the troop draws nigh,
When 'midst them I am seen to stand,
And gladly reach to him my hand.

THE WORK-GIRL.

Now merry cricket, sing thy lay,
Until the wick is burnt away,
And I may to my bed repair
And dream about my sweetheart there.

I sit and spin, but cannot get
Half through the skein of wool as yet;
When I shall spin it out, God knows,
Or when the tardy eve will close!

THE PEASANT YOUTH.

I'VE hewed and hewed again the wood,
   Till all my strength is gone;
The axe's steel is sharp and good,
   And yet the fir stands on.

My arm was once both stark and strong,
   But is so now no more,
Since bark I eat all winter long,
   And water drank thereo'er.

If I should change my service now,
   A better one to try,
Perhaps a master I might know
   Who gave me bread of rye.

Mayhap I in the town might get
   For faithful work some pay,
So have I often thought, and yet
   I cannot yearn that way.

Does there the mountain's leaf-decked rise
  In mirrored lakes appear?
Does there the glorious sun arise
  And set as mild as here?

And are there dales with fragrance fraught,
  And moors that pine-trees bear?
And she, whose horn my ear just caught,
  Will she, too, meet me there?

The clouds unsheltered fly and come,
  The sport of every wind,
What is a life, when foster-home
  And friends are left behind?

Perhaps God hears what people pray,
  And lightens troubles sore,
Perhaps the autumn's harvest may
  Have better bread in store.

THE ROWER.

SING now, poor boy, sing now,
　Lest wearily thou row,
Soon faints thy hand upon the oar,
Then who shall speed the boat ashore?

No wave moves on the sea,
Of sun and day, I see
The merest streak in western skies,
Dark in the firth the dim cloud lies.

But say, poor fellow, say,
Where hastenest thou away?
Alone and tired in toilsome quest,
With night e'en gone, to soothing rest.

Were those some wild fowl there,
Thou by the strand didst scare? .
A diver, or a duck, art thou
From strand to strand pursuing now?

Thou, who from wooded heights
Hast asked me many nights,
Dost ask me now, hast asked before:
Hear, echo, my reply once more!

It was no wild-fowl there
I by the strand did scare,
No diver, and no duck do I
From strand to strand pursuing fly.

My thought I'm hunting for;
With each stroke of the oar,
However light or faint, I'm brought
Still nearer onward to my thought.

Lo, where the smoke goes up
Against yon rock's blue top,
There shows the hut, yon marshes o'er,
Whither my thought is gone before.

There shall I find it then,
When, e'er 'tis day again,
The boat has reached the harbour's rest,
And I, my faithful maiden's breast.

THE PINE-THRUSH.

SO free, at last, one breathes and moves once more,
   No scorching Sun doth now its sheen down-pour;
No remnant of the summer's day to show,
But, glaring through the grove, the western glow,
And of the wind a faint and cooling gale,
Which soon shall die upon our flowery dale.

Thou, friend of silv'ry evening, only thou,
Oh pine-thrush, break'st the country's silence now!
Let day be fiery, balmy be the night,
Of both thou borrow'st poetry's colours bright;
And paintest in imperishable song
Thy faith's high festival all springtime long.

Thou hast, like me, a friend to whom to tell
The joy, the pain that makes thy soft heart swell.
Have I, like thee, such an harmonious mood,—
A speech as tender, as well understood?
Oh, can I tell how deep my love is now,
Or ever love as tenderly as thou?

THE PINE-THRUSH.

Oh, happy he, whom nature's very breast
Doth with his love, and words, and voice invest,
Who, wandering, ne'er forgets his mother-speech,
He dreameth but, his dreams alone doth teach;
Unconscious, with no rules to bind his tongue,
He dreameth wisdom, and he speaketh song.

I'll listen by the wood's edge, Scald, to thee,
Till from the evening clouds the glow shall flee,
And till night's torch its pale sheen lights again;
My maid will meet me by the cottage then.
And, should I tell her how I felt thy tone,
I use no words, but kiss on kiss alone.

THE YOUNG HUNTSMAN.

OUT in the fields but birds are met,
   And leaves grow dim anon,
I have not made a shot as yet,
   And eve is coming on.

If winter would but once come back
   With snowdrift, I should see
Much better then the grouse to track,
   Black-cock would keep the tree.

If but the air would cooler grow,
   And leaves would fall again,
The nearest dale, perhaps, might show
   A heath-cock covey then.

Yet soon the grouse's track will show,
   The heath-cock's cover be o'er,
Her whom I most would look on, though,
   Shall I see none the more.

I'm looking here, she's looking there,
   But ah, I meet her not,
I might stand in the glance of her,
   And yet behold her not.

Between us there is mount and main,
   And moors with many a tree,
Between us, day and eve again,
   And night, too, it may be.

THE MORNING.

SOME few drops of purple blush the
   Sun o'er Eastern clouds hath spread,
And on blade and bud and bush the
   Pearly shower of dew is shed.

Woodland's every bird is flying
   Blithe from top to top around;
Sounds of joy, by thousands dying,
   Thousandfold again resound.

Creased the firth, a crisp wave swelleth,
   Woods with breeze on breeze awake,
Life and flowery fragrance dwelleth
   In each single breath we take.

Angel from afar on high and
   Every being's friend, has yet,
Dawn! a single gloomy eye and
   Thine own lustrous aspect met?

M.

Scattered trouble's fogs are flying,
  Dismal clouds of thought are gone;
Day, in hours of childhood lying,
  Childhood's feelings loves alone.

Nothing suffers, nothing yearneth,
  All is gladness, peace, and hope;
And as nature's morn returneth,
  Every bosom's morn doth ope.

THE KISS.

I'M kissing thee, nor weary grow,
And shall I ever weary? No.
Now, darling maiden, answer me,
What bliss a kiss doth give to thee?

Thou lovest it as well as I;
Say, wherein does its pleasure lie?
I ask now, asked thee lately, this,
And get for answer kiss on kiss!

If in my lip did honey lie,
Thou could'st not kiss more tenderly;
Did even gall thereon distill,
Yet would'st thou kiss as fondly still.

See here, what plea canst thou adduce,
If any ask thee thine excuse,
If any, pertly coming now,
Should ask thee, wherefore kissest thou?

THE KISS.

Folk judge severely, dear, now pray,
What will they of a person say
Who kisses, and does nothing more,
And does not know herself what for?

For my part, I could never see
What good in kissing there might be.
But I will die ere aught shall keep
Me from thy lips of crimson deep.

REGRET.

KEEP in thy faithful lap, oh, poplar shade, here
  The vows, which at his meeting last he made here,
His bold entreaties, ire, unrest endearing,
Were but for silence, for mine and thine hearing.

Already from on high the sun had glided,
And not a star her eyelids yet divided,
Nowhere a breath of wind abroad was starting,
When he 'gan struggling for my kiss at parting.

To thee alone can I tell what concerned me,
How every sigh, each tear he shed then, burned me,
How thousand kisses I had given contented,
Had not my maiden modesty prevented.

Tell him, thou, if at any time he stroll here,
To dream awhile beside thee in the cool here;
Tell him, if language thou commandest ever,
The words, I trembling now to thee deliver.

"Forget, good youth, what gave thee pain and smart here,
The cold she feigned was far, far from her heart here;
Let not her seeming cold with ire inspire thee,
Nor ever let her coy caprices tire thee."

THAT WAS THEN.

HIGH on the sand there
   Swelleth the angry sea;
Birch on the strand there
   Speaks no more green to me;
   Stark is the snowy lea.

Fledst thou with spring the
   Dale from thy friends away,
Could tears but bring thee
   Back, for an hour to stay,
   Then I to thee would say:

"Look round the leas here,
   Girl, once again, for thou
Mindest the trees here,
   Once green and sweet? But how
   'Are they appearing now?"

Then she, in going,
  Would say to me again :
"Fairer was glowing,
  Fair youth, thy cheek too, when
  That was! Ah, that was then!"

THE SAILOR'S GIRL.

NOW the wind is freshening fast,
  Sails are filling, yard and mast,
Forth the craft to far lands steereth;
God knows, when it reappeareth.

Thou, who sailest there, canst thou
Spare a look for me, e'en now?
Thee I might in sight be keeping
Still, could I but stanch my weeping.

Oh, if like the bird I were,
Winged, as is the sea-mew there!
I would follow o'er the waters,
To the wide world's unknown quarters.

Always come, where thou should'st come,
Turn, when thou returnedst home,
With my light wing play before thee,
Catch thy glance in hovering o'er thee.

All that a poor maid can do,
Is to wave thee an adieu,
Tear-filled kerchief in her hand here,
Wingless left upon the strand here.

With no chance to follow so,
I again must homeward go,
Ere the evening twilight neareth,
Ere the sail e'en disappeareth.

From my breast must chase the grief,
Though it be my sole relief,
On my cheek the tears must smother,
Lest their trace be seen by Mother.

GREETING.

SKIES are clearing up, dull showers are leaving
   Room for evening's sunshine now to peep;
On the firth, upon a sea-swell heaving,
   Day-time's storm is rocked and lulled to sleep.

She who for me long her watch was keeping,
   Sees not yet my wherry thither steer,
Stands she, may be, on the sea-shore weeping,
   Gazing hither, may be, with a tear.

Not a gust to fill my sail there cometh,
   Though I row, she'll make but little way;
And far o'er the glassy inlet loometh
   Yonder cape where my beloved doth stay.

Swallow, thou so fond of flight and flutter,
   With a message fly my love to cheer,
On her shoulder, seen by no one, utter
   These my words and slip them in her ear.

"Darling girl, if for thy love thou 'rt yearning,
  Hear his faithful greeting now through me;
When the wind but wakes with morn returning,
  Will he loose his boat and come to thee.

Far away, he needs himself, thy lover,
  Help from wind o'er firth and sound to scour;
But, however calm, like me, thereover
  Lightly swoops his Thought to thee each hour.

Song-bird's notes within the woods awaking,
  Rills among the strand-fells murm'ring, but
Only midge-swarms' airy pinions quaking,
  Waft it, quick as light'ning, to thy hut."

MIND—FOR THEN THE GOD APPEARETH.

PRETTY maiden, sportive fairy,
    Wait a few more summers barely,
And thou shalt not look so airy,
    And shalt be so gleeful rarely!

Only gladness fourteen reareth,
    Fifteen goes and sixteen fleetly,
With his flame the god appeareth,
    And the thing is changed completely.

One spark of his fire a-glowing
    Saddened thoughts by thousands breedeth;
From his bow one flutter bloweth—
    And the freshest heart e'en bleedeth.

Calm is broken, joy infected,
    Choice no pleasures follow after,
And within the eye reflected
    Pain is seen 'twixt hope and laughter.

Maiden 'gainst his painful darts then
　Anxious watch as yet is needless;
For the God comes nigh no hearts when
　Still their instinct slumbers heedless.

But when peace to yearning turneth,
　Yearning to desire that teareth,
Mind,—his sleep the sleeper spurneth;
　Mind—for then the God appeareth.

SERENADE.

WITHIN my maiden's bower no lamp there flareth,
But pale-red moonlight on the window glareth,
I see now,—through the curtain drawn thereo'er,—
    The fair one's form no more.

Soon to her couch's refuge safe retreating
Watch her, oh, bashful Cynthia, then, repeating,
In kindly guise, what thou didst chance to see,
    But to the Night and me.

If with a look, whence heaven's lustre peepeth,
She folds her hands together then and weepeth,
And words, but heard by Angels, she betrays,
    'Tis evening prayer she says.

But should her breast heave throbbing 'neath its cover,
About her rosy lips should laughter hover,
And should her cheek's flame gently kindled be—
    Then dreameth she of me.

DISSIMULATION.

All know pleasures and distresses,
   Though not all may talk about it;
Every maid a heart possesses,
   Though she feigns to be without it.

Joys, that gods to men are giving,
   May, they know not when, surprise them;
Kisses loves each maiden living,
   Though she feigneth to despise them.

Love, oh, youth, with ardour burn, and
   Then with cold thou'lt be requited;
Strike a path of unconcern, and
   With thy pain thy Belle is freighted.

And the vainly hid distresses
   Say through looks and voice about it:
"Every maid a heart possesses,
   Though she feigns to be without it."

Claim a thousand kisses,—all she
 Grants, while she compulsion feigneth;
Claim thou none,—though cold withal, she
 Not from even one abstaineth :—

Through her tears in looks oft giveth
 Forth the words, and softly sighs them:
"Kisses loves each maid that liveth,
 Though she feigneth to despise them!"

BUTTERFLY AND ROSE.

PALE of cheek the rose is stooping,
    And her time is past;
And the butterfly is drooping
    'Neath the showery blast.
When shall butterfly recover
Her amusements and her lover?
    When shall wane the
    Trance again, the
Rose's languid eyes unlock?

Babes of summer, both were living
    Like it, happily;
Neither shifts nor dangers giving
    Trouble to their glee.
With each other's kiss elated,
With no debts unexpiated,
    Unmolested
    Both had rested,
Yet must feel vexation's shock.

How they tarry, how they bide now,
   Waking never more!
Not e'en Love with Spring beside now
   Can their life restore.
Yet the knoll, where each reposes,
Showeth fresh and lovely roses.
     To the balm there
     O'er dust's calm there
Fresh-born butterflies now flock.

THE BIRD-CATCHER.

I WALK along the woodland ways,
   And up in fir and pine I gaze,
And oft enough the birds I see,
But none fly near to me.

They all appear to fly away
Where'er my trap I chance to lay,
And empty-handed, as I come,
I have to wend towards home.

I ought to see with grief and dread
How badly has my fowling sped.
But let it fail me as it will,
I am contented still.

THE BIRD CATCHER.

One snare, I still have left behind,
I never yet did empty find,
As glad the bird for it will make,
As I the same shall take.

And when, to-night, my home is made,
For that bird shall my trap be laid,
That bird's name is my girl—my lap
Is that bird's very trap.

TO THE EVENING STAR.

STAR, the evening's daughter, thou,
   Say, what thou beholdest now!
Seest thou from thy stronghold there
More of gladness or despair?

Sailors on a stormy sea
From the billows' grave, may be,
Now with fear and now with hope,
Eyes towards thy guidance ope.

And in some forgotten dale,
Lonely left there with its bale,
Now a broken heart may seek
Comfort in thine eye so meek.

TO THE EVENING STAR.

May be, that to thee, e'en now
Lifts some faithful maid her brow,
With a steadfast gaze and prayer,
To detect her lover there.

If thou seest a sail astray,
Set it right upon its way,
Seest thou grief suppressed, forgot,
Grudge thy beaming comfort not.

But shouldst thou my girl survey,
Send her down a friendly ray,
And then write its sheen among :
That I've waited here so long.

THE DYING MAN.

THE weary night will very soon be passed;
  Is not the heaven bright and clear at last?
Does not the marsh-snow brighter still appear?
Is't not the black-cock's cry that now I hear?

When, very soon, the morning sun shall glow,
And on the roof begins to melt the snow,
And when drop after drop I shall descry
Fall past the open window by and by,

And when the cricket grows still, and I hear
The merry sparrow outside twittering near,
Then, let me pray you, make me a fresh bed:
A wisp of straw, upon the hall-steps spread.

For I would there be led, would rest me there,
To see how glad is nature and how fair;
And joyous cast o'er land and sea my eye,
And then in spring-time, where I lived, would die.

THE YOUTH.

WIND that caressest and veerest,
    Say, whither is it thou steerest,
Shiftily swift fleeting there,
Say, where thou harbourest,—where?

Billow, that rockest my prore now,
Followed I thee with my oar now
On with thy drift, in thy wake,
Answer, what port should I make?

Thoughts, without number, oh, say ye,
Where drop you anchor?—The way ye,
Children of nobler worlds, wend,
Unto a goal does it tend?

TO A ROSE.

SLUMBERER, in the pent-up bud represséd,
    Waken soon, thy foster-dale to charm!
Kissed by butterflies, by drops caresséd,
    Which from heaven are falling cool and calm.

Hasten, hasten, all the moment giveth,
    Only for the moment's reign can last:
Hasten, hasten, joy like life but liveth,
    Life is spring again but fleeting fast.

Love, enjoy thyself, and glow fair flower,
    Open out thy beauty more and more!
May an angel come, ere autumn lower,
    Break thee off, and to thy heaven restore.

THE BELLE.

All is good that I endeavour,
  Easy that for which I care;
All they whisper to me ever
  Is, that I am fair.

Now they praise my glances' fire,
  Now my growth, or colors bright,—
Could I not my glass inquire,
  Or believe my sight?

Noting what the glass discovers,
  I myself can see of me
More than all the crowd of lovers
  In one evening see.

Sweet to be with praise regarded,
  Although praise is nought but air;
Should my heart be disregarded
  For my cheek though fair?

Yet the cheek alone is noted,
  But by that is passion led;
And by none a word devoted
  To my heart is said.

BY A FOUNTAIN.

OH, fountain, on thy bank I stand,
    And watch the cloud-troops' drift,
How, led on by an unseen hand,
    Within thy wave they shift.

There came a cloud, it laughed as red
    As rosebuds laugh and burn.—
Farewell, how soon farewell it said,
    To nevermore return.

Another, brighter still, adrift,
    Of still more beaming hue!
Ah, just as fleeting, just as swift
    Does that one vanish, too!

And now another,—'twill not fly,
    It sails on heavily;
But fountain, it bedims the sky,
    And it has darkened thee.

My thoughts, when I behold thee so,
   On my own soul must dwell;
How many a golden cloud also
   Has bidden it farewell!

How many a dark and dull one spread
   Its night thereon, and then,
Though coming quickly, ah! it sped
   So slowly off again.

But how they came, and how they fled,
   I knew them well:—the whole
Were merely clouds, that overspread
   The mirror of my soul.

And yet the mirror's light and shade
   Must on these clouds depend!—
Oh, fount, when is this game out-played,
   Thy wave's unrest at end?

THE MAID OF SEVENTEEN.

I KNOW not what I hope for,
   Yet hope I none the less;
My heart it feels so empty,
Yet fills to such excess.
Where tendeth this disquiet,
That ne'er its goal hath won?
What wish I for, what will I,
What do I think upon?

Like any drudge at sewing
I sit the livelong day;
I seem to work in earnest,
Yet time wears not away.
My head sinks on my hand, with
My needle-work 'tis done;
What wish I for, what will I,
What do I think upon?

I thought, when only spring comes
With nature freshly dight,
Then will my mind be altered,
My troubles take their flight.
But, spring-time came, and summer,
While I the same kept on.
What wish I for, what will I,
What do I think upon?

The lovely country's charms now
I love not as before.
The more the days are brightening
My gloom grows all the more;
What will disperse my unrest,
When will my grief be gone?
What wish I for, what will I,
What do I think upon?

Oh, he, who may repose in
Death's tranquil home, is blest!
May be 'tis but the grave, where
The heart doth find its rest.
And yet, how sad, already
To leave both friends and sun.
What wish I for, what will I,
What do I think upon?

THE REVENGE.

BRIGHT and fair the brook is leaping,
   Now in silver, now in gold;
Through the sultry hedge are peeping
   Languid roses manifold.

By the brook's cool wave invited
   Come the maidens from the lea;
'Mid the hedge-leaves close united
   Lies a youth hid purposely.

No one's eye sees aught the matter,
   No one's wanton tongue is bound;
But to mirth the damsels scatter
   Thousand giddy gifts around.

"Fancy but, if some one hears now
   All our fun and merry shout!"
"Fancy, if the hedge had ears now!"
   Cries the youth, and boundeth out.

Him to chase and catch we hasten!
  He is soon no longer free.
Him we bind and him we chasten,
  Bound and chastened hard is he.

Guess, what were his fetters wrought of?
  All of roses linked and wound.
Guess, what punishment they thought of?
  'Twas to kiss the girls all round.

THE FLOWER'S LOT.

'MONG summer's babes I saw a rose one day
    In the beginning of its flowery lease,
With purple cheek lapped in the bud it lay,
    And dreamt but of its innocence and peace.

"Thou pretty floweret, wake, thine eye lift up,
    With life's sweet lot thyself to satisfy,"
Said, fluttering over leaf and flower-cup,
    The wanton gold-besprinkled butterfly.

"See, dark and poor appears thy dwelling slight,
    And reft of joy thy heart is beating there;
Here gladness liveth, gloweth day's broad light,
    And here await thee love and kisses fair."

Upon the floweret's soul the speech did tell,
    Soon to the flatterer she her mouth lay bare,
The butterfly then kissed her;—bade farewell!
    And to fresh rose-buds swiftly did repair.

WHO HITHER STEERED THY WAY?

FAR o'er the firth away,
  Far off across the fell,
Alone thou sawest day,
  Grewst up alone as well.

For thee I never yearned,
  Thy way I never sought,
No path I ever learned,
  That might have thither brought.

Thy father knew I not,
  Did not thy mother know,
I never saw the spot
  Where thou didst come and go.

E'en as the brook that flowed
  Before that flowing there,
While that was thine abode,
  We for each other were.

Two plants 'twixt which is laid
   A meadow full of flowers,
Two birds whose home is made
   In sundered woodland bowers.

Son of another land,
   Why thence thou fleddest, say!
O bird from far-off strand,
   Who hither steered thy way?

Unto a chilly heart
   A flame how hast thou brought!
How is't that all thou art,
   To whom thou wert as nought!

THE BRIDE.

IF I saw thee, if I saw thee nearing,
   Steering round the foreland's birches there,
Saw the sail first, then descried the veering
   Purple-bunting, thou for flag dost bear.

If some glad lines thou didst bring me rather,
   From thy sister, when thou mad'st for this,
If with "Yes" thou camest from thy father,
   From thy mother with a mother's kiss!

Why put off our bliss? the years will bring in
   Gold and goods, thou may'st be sure of it.
Love is like the floweret, and in Spring, in
   Spring alone, it finds a season fit.

Hasten, hills are bright, and dales green growing,
   Like the birds' our bliss grows there as well.
E'en in alder tree-tops scorched and glowing
   I quite happily with thee could dwell.

REGRET.

WITHIN the woods is left no bough,
    Doth leaves and beauty bear;
The summer has departed now,
    Here is but wintry air.

Yes, out of doors doth winter show,
    And all indoors doth fill,
And should I to the world's end go,
    I should behold it still.

Let woods be green and warm the plain,
    Let day be bright and clear,
In my breast would the cold remain
    As ever chill and drear.

Thee, joy and sunlight of mine eyes,
    They shall no more adore;
Sun of my heart, thou wilt arise
    From out the grave no more.

My soul was thine, my feeling thine,
   Thy life was life for me;
Except regret now nought is mine,
   The rest has gone with thee.

'Tis best that, hushed, the hearth beside,
   My past days I review,
When fires burn low and eventide
   Has left me nought to do.

SPRING DITTY.

THEY'RE coming, they're coming,
    The winged crowds that erst from us flew,
To groves, that are blooming,
    To lakes, that are thawing anew.

Where storm-winds were flying,
    Sounds song now, melodious and sweet;
Where snow-drifts were lying,
    Have gladness and beauty their seat.

'Tis but love arrests here
    From clouds'-tracts the fugitive band,
And heaven's own guests here
    Seek only a bright-smiling land.

My heart shall be blooming,
    My feelings be thawing anew,
Mayhap, they are coming,
    The angels, that erst from me flew.

TO FORTUNE.

FORTUNE, goddess ever smiling,
    Born to make the hour sweet,
Not thee Queen of this earth styling
    Does my lyre thy presence greet.
Without triumph, without guile, too,
    With no power, no crown to show,
Thy mild aim's to reconcile to
    Dust all mankind here below.

Hail thee, for no heart e'er bleedeth
    'Neath thy guarding hand that stands:
Brother it to brother leadeth,
    Over desert, fell, and lands.
Wind in Longing's sails thou blowest,
    Dost reward the faithful breast;
Shadowed in thy mirror showest
    Thou the world of higher rest.

TO FORTUNE.

Why as false should folk belie thee,
   Though thou fail'st now and again?
Couldst thou but to all ally thee,
   None would be forgotten then.
Now, how couldst thou join together
   All that in its fall did break?
One thou must leave, while another
   Thou thy favourite dost make.

Light's allotment, Peace' donation,
   Hope and love and joyfulness,
All that has life's adoration
   I possessed and still possess.
Thee I aye saw disappearing,
   When securing hold on thee,—
Dust's mild goddess, weak and veering,
   Smile also for once on me!

THE HEART'S MORNING.

DARKNESS swayed my mind each minute,
   Cold my poor heart felt and blighted,
Till love's fervour was within it
   By a friendly angel lighted.

Seest the sun from Night's dark quarter
   Sweep across the heavens beaming,
Gloom is scattered, land and water
   In a saintly halo gleaming.

Seest the image of my heart then—
   Thus its early morn upstarted,
Thus with fear, and void, and smart then
   From its world the shades departed.

THE HEARTS' MORNING.

Sun, dispelling life's night dreary,
  Love, if breasts knew nought about thee,
What for are those days so weary
  Which are dreamt away without thee,

Days for aye the same subsisting,
  Hours to hopeless length extended,
Life in death's domain existing,
  With no light, no marvel blended!

THE DOUBTER.

OH had I but of eyes a pair
   That keener than the falcon's were,
A glance from checks and dimness free,
Through height and depth and space to see.

No pearl, the best the sea can yield,
No jewel in Earth's night concealed,
No seam of gold in rocky nook,
For none of these my eye should look.

Upon her heart I'd keep my view
And look the false maid through and through,
The false one playing me the fool,
Now soft and sweet, now hard and cool.

Is cold within her breast, perchance,
When sweet and warm appears her glance?
Is love hid in its depth, when she
Appears to look most freezingly?

For prayerful sighs doth heaven ope,
For sorrow's self hath earth some hope,
For me, it is my love's sad doom
To doubt, and doubting to consume.

THE BRIDE.

Come, gentle stranger, take thine ease,
   And at my hut alight,
Stir not the silent country's peace
   Upon this quiet night;
To sorrow is its stillness dear,
A broken heart is watching here.

See, on the inlet's naked strand,
   A maid beholdest thou;
Her forehead rested on her hand,
   She sits there lonely now,
And silent looks o'er land and creek,
And white as is the snow her cheek.

She many a day, oh, many a night,
   Was seen there to repair;
Yestre'en she sat there by the bight,
   To-morrow finds her there.
Erewhile a stray tear would she show,
But now she has wept out long ago.

THE BRIDE.

When evening cometh soft and bright,
   The breeze flies forth apace,
And, like a glass, the bay shows bright
   A heaven in its face;
Then sinks upon the water's ways
Her rigid look to gaze and gaze.

And when again the wind awakes,
   The billow's face is stirred,
The gleam grows rough, the mirror breaks,
   The deep's bright heaven is blurred.
Then lifts the silent one her eye,
And looks up hopeless to the sky.

She once sat on that very strand,
   Looked o'er that very bay,
She saw her lover leave the land,
   And hither wend his way.
By yon cliff was the sea his grave,
Nor ever back his body gave.

Her dreary quiet to molest,
   Oh, stranger, then forbear!
And leave her grieving gaze to rest
   Upon her deep sea there.
It is the only joy now left
Of all whereof she once was reft.

M.

THE SUNDAY HARVEST.

HIGH beaming morning's sun is seen,
    And nature dons light's lustrous sheen;
With song-birds' notes resoundeth space,
And no one stirs yet in the place.

Why rests the farmer still in bed?
Is day not bright again o'er head,
Ripe fields and tilth their wealth unfold,
What makes him then despise their gold?

But see, he opes his cot e'en now,
How calm, how blissful looks his brow,
Oppressive cares that on him weigh,
He like a robe has cast away.

No tools upon his arm bears he,
His breast is light, his shoulder free,
Nor do his hands the sickle ply,
Although the harvest-home draws nigh.

THE SUNDAY HARVEST.

At length the feast hath come about,
And child and mate he summons out;
And with them goes devout his way
Now to the harvest of the day.

And glad he sees, how him before
The crowds are gathering more and more,
And friends and strangers seek apace
The selfsame goal, the selfsame place :—

Unto the whitened walls, that there
The cross of holy peace up-bear;
Unto the very golden field,
That doth the eternal harvest yield.

THE OLD MAN.

A KING, meseems, the old man shows,
  Approaching life's long pathway's close,
His journey's goal at last to see
Triumphant, enviable he!

Time's every storm already spent,
His might gains neighbours' glad assent;
And errors bold, and passions gay,
From his still realm fly far away.

His people are a peaceful crowd
Of wishes soft in slumber's shroud,
Of memories which within him stay
From old and sweetly by-gone day.

His sceptre is his pilgrim's stave,
His burgh, his strong burgh, is his grave,
His royal pomp, his tranquil air,
His crown, his very silver hair.

THE FLOWER.

WHEN the spring once more is showing
   Sweet and clear,
Day is laughing, sunlight glowing—
   Wak'st thou here;
On thy soft stem givest birth to
   Bud and sprout,
Like an angel seek'st from earth to
   Struggle out.

With thy scent the breeze that blows then
   Onward cleaves,
Gold-winged butterflies repose then
   On thy leaves.
With thy cheek dares no uncleanness
   Kissing play,—
Dew, wind, butterflies, sereneness—
   Only they.

Since, like plants when summer cometh
  Mild and fair,
All that's sweet is born and bloometh
  Without care,
Why should grief and danger go here
  Hand in hand?—
Why is not our earth below here
  Peace's land?

AUTUMN SONG.

Foliage paleth,
   Trees their raiment shed,
And November gloom prevaileth
   O'er dead flowers' bed.
Snowy drifts their crowns have blighted;
But in hearts whom they delighted,
While the summer's warmth did still remain,
They revive as memories again.

Roses flower,
   For a few days' span;
But outlasts their summer's hour
   Thy flower's lease, oh, man?
Fair it shooteth forth and gleameth,
Glows its cheek, its bright eye beameth;
But against its stem a breeze there flies,
And it fades, and stoops, and shrinks, and dies.

Thou, who didst wake me
  Out of earth's dark night,
Mid thy flower-creation make me
  Sprout forth pure and bright.
That though summer's sun ignore me,
Some kind angel may have for me
'Mong the memories he from earth shall bear
One, too, of my quiet blooming there.

COMING HOME.

LONE sheen, afar,
   Flame, pure as that of a star,
  Light from my father's hearth hurled,
Art thou still twinkling, so late?
  Happy, harmonious world,
Dost thou the wand'rer await?

  Day is all told,
Dark is my pathway and cold,
  Drear in the woods, where I fare,
Winter, the icy, is king;
  Light, where thou twinklest, oh, there
Find I my love and my spring.

  Haste on thy way,
Fortunate!—thou mayest some day,
  Mute, when thy wandering is o'er,
This home parental perceive.
  Light is thy dwelling no more,
Chilly and lonesome thine eve.

MY LIFE.

STRUGGLING o'er an open grave,
　Sailing o'er an angry wave,
Toiling on with aimless aim,
Oh, my life, I name thy name!

Longing fills the sailor's soul,
Seas before his eyesight roll,
"Lo, behind yon purple haze
"Higher sights shall meet my gaze.

"I shall near a better strand,
"Light and freedom's happy land."—
Swelled the sail, expectance laughed,
Towards the Boundless sped the craft.

Struggling o'er an open grave,
Sailing o'er an angry wave,
Toiling on with aimless aim,
Oh, my life, I name thy name!

Ah, the haven calm and clear,
Peace of heart in by-gone year,
Hope's gold coast, ah! hidden spot,
Never reached, and ne'er forgot!

Billows check the sailor's course,
Over-head the tempest hoarse:—
Still is yonder purple haze
Far as ever from his gaze!

THOUGHT.

THOUGHT, see birds, that lightly swing and
   Freely 'neath the cloudy sky,
Even thou hast got thy wing, and
   Thine own space, wherein to fly.

Fret not, that to dust's low site thou
   As a prisoner tied shouldst be;
Light as bird, and swift as light, thou
   Art than either still more free.

If 'tis glad on earth, then rest thee,
   'Mong its pleasures glad also;
If 'tis sad, then haste thee, haste thee,
   Forth to higher worlds to go.

THE FORSAKEN.

HERBS and leaflets and flowerets small,
Lilies light and bedewed withal,
Damask rose with the smile benign,
For my bridal will I entwine;
Forget-me-not by the ripples clear,
Ne'er a thorn-growth thy stem doth rear,
How unlike unto thee it shows,
Which e'en now in my bosom grows,
Which has prickles in every part,
And which only so wounds my heart.

Sing my bridal-song, brooklet, sing,
Gentle fountain, and water-spring,
Sing ye glad of the days in store,
That the past I may mind no more,
Mind not life with its pain and play,
Mind not who did my faith betray.

Sing my bridal-song, brooklet, sing,
Gentle fountain and water-spring.
Softly sing ye my own soul through
To the false one a long adieu.

I will choose me another love,
Will not lightly so traitorous prove,
Will not kiss me while spring doth last,
But to vanish when it is passed;
Come, oh, death, take this heart of mine,
Let it rest now to-day on thine,
Though thy bride be with weeping blind,
Pale of cheek though thy maid thou find,
Though thy rose no more red should be,
Come, oh, death, come, sweet death, to me.

AUTUMN EVENING.

How bleak is all, how wasted, withered, dead!
   Where is the bloom now, which the summer fed?
The dale is numbed, each woodland sound abated,
And for a grave dull earth is consecrated.

Yet from the grave in bliss the eye doth ope,
A higher world dawns for the heart's fond hope.
Earth's twilight forth the starlands' sheen beguileth,
A home untransient to the spirit smileth.

Thus dream I in the autumn eve, and see,
How stark the foliage falls down from the tree.
A naked strand doth yon bay's deep discover,
And o'er the moon the silver cloudlets hover.

WAITING.

MOTHER minds her household cares,
    At her sewing sister keeps,
And ahunting brother goes,
But myself with cheek on hand
I am sitting dreaming here.
Oh, my lover, where art thou,
Not yet traced, not e'en yet known,
Only yearned and waited for?

MEMORY.

ONCE more in the solitude a visit
    From departed friends, dear and lamented,
From the figures of my blissful season;
Lake by cottage, cottage, woodland, mountain,
My amusements, my enjoyments, visions,
And my first love's sighing in its blossom!
Oh, I ponder upon nature's goodness,
That amidst regret she grants us memory,
Which the past time's bliss so sweet and cooling,
Like a morning-dew the heart sheds over,
Even when the mid-day's sun is burning.

THE PAINTER.

THOU wishest for a place within my rhymes now,
  Dear maiden, thou hast asked me a thousand times now,
To try in tints poetical to trace,
Some idle day, the features of thy face.

My pencil shall be spared no more, however;
Choose but the hour, and, while thou sitt'st, endeavour
In look, demeanour, temper and in form
To mine, the artist's, orders to conform.

Be beautiful! 'tis beauty's proper part, but
To be united to the soul of art;—but
A maid is beautiful, when glad and gay;
Be therefore glad, whene'er I come thy way.

Be tender! for though much thy beauty weigheth,
Yet winning grace the heart alone displayeth;
Fix therefore ever, for the sake of grace,
A look of fire and love upon my face.

And goodness in the picture should be lying:
Desire for giving, soothing, gratifying.
Whenever idle, then, forget not this,
To stretch thy purple mouth out for a kiss.

Fair, tender, good, what glow would fire thy stature!
Yet slightly selfish should be painters' nature:
And, therefore, say, whene'er I draw a line,
That thou for ever, ever wilt be mine.

THE TWO.

IN the palace-halls are gleaming
   Thousand lamps, like sunlight blazing,
And 'midst floods of light are streaming
   Odours delicate, amazing.

All is ordered, guests are coming
   Who o'er fortune's summits hover,
Autumns wither, springs are blooming,
   Whom both gold and jewels cover.

Silence deep awhile falls o'er them
   All, as though for prayers preparing,
Till the hero steps before them,
   Every eye upon him staring.

'Tis the groom, in stars redundant,
   Orders gay his costume weighting;
With her heaven of bliss abundant
   For the fair bride he is waiting.

And she cometh with her father;
  See her, at his gentle leading,
Midst the noble guests that gather,
  To her bridegroom's side proceeding.

Is she happy, can she feel now
  Any earthly blessing wanted?
Can a wish itself reveal now,
  Which is not already granted?

Ah, she stands there pallid, taking
  Little heed of all the splendour;
'Neath her crown her locks are quaking,
  Tears her eye o'erclouded render.

To the marriage-questions spoken,
  But her lip the Yes replieth,
Thought and being both betoken
  That she far, far off abieth.

Outside of the palace swells a
  Sea upon the lonely skerry,
With their wreath of firs the fells a
  Murky night in gloom doth bury.

THE TWO.

On the rocks all foam-bestrown there
   Canst thou see a spectre straying?
In the chilly eve alone there
   May'st thou see a young man staying.

Autumn's storm-cloud onward presses,
   Yet no way the youth recedeth;
Dew, congealing in his tresses,
   As a thing of nought he heedeth.

And the sea's white surf-spray, streaming
   O'er the fells, upon him playeth,
Oh, he goes on with his dreaming,
   'Tis his shade alone that stayeth.

Oh, when heart as heart is, mark there,
   'Twixt the two what oneness showeth;
See him in the night so dark there,
   Her in halls where splendour gloweth.

Nightly darkness, daylight's flame then,
   All that cheereth, all that paineth,
Is it not one and the same then,
   When life's root a hurt sustaineth?

THE VAIN WISH.

UNNUMBERED the billows wander
  About the sea's glistening way,
Oh, were I but with them yonder,
  A wave in the ocean astray!
So deeply indifferent-minded,
  So carelessly chilly and clear,
So utterly unreminded
  Of bygone blissfuller year!

Yet, were I a billow roving,
  The same as I am should I show,
For here in a crowd I am moving
  Of chilly billows also.
With pleasure and pain they are gaming,
  They weep and make merry for play,
But I have my heart all aflaming,
  Oh, were I but outside as they.

IN A YOUNG GIRL'S ALBUM.

WARM the spring-sun in the heaven glowed,
    Gleamed the fields with dew and insects swarming,
On the mead a youthful violet shewed;
    Know'st thou what she thought, that floweret charming?

Why, she thought: "How lovely, here to live,
    Here to charm, hope, laugh, enjoy for ever;
Thou who light and hue to me didst give,
    Let my blooming never finish, never!"

So she prayed, was it an idle prayer?
    Was it joy or grief that she was seeking?
Was she, praying to be young and fair,
    Of her heart or of her cheek then speaking?

Like the floweret pray, thou, flower also!
    Life and charms life's angel loveth dearly;
Pray thou then, but for thy flower-soul, so,
    For thy floweret-stem is transient merely.

TO THE LADIES.

THE youth, when he his greeting bringeth you,
　　With soul on fire, with brow that garlands weareth,
Awards the prize unto your cheeks' fair hue:
　　His homage to their bloom; while our's another shareth.
We also love life's springtime's splendours gay,
　　But such, as shall endure, when springs have fled away.

Years more than his have our experience made,
　　Their gifts like wind are changing every hour.
While best it burns the meadow-flower will fade,
　　No other fate awaits the cheeks' fair flower.
Who loved it not what day its smiles it wore?
　　But still there comes a day, when it is seen no more.

TO THE LADIES.

There is a flower to which we homage own,
  A healing herb for pain as well as pleasure.
Its name is Love; which coy, not glittering, grown
  And nursed in patience, is your warm hearts'
                              treasure.
Where it can heal, there first it comes to sight,
  So sweet, though earnest, and in weakness full of
                              might.

For joy and cheer, from cradle to our grave,
  From days that are gone by, to days still coming,
For all the tears that it has dried, we have
  To own our homage to this hidden flower blooming:
This shoot, a seedling of eternity,
  Oh, never leave it here to fade, or shrink, or die.

IDYLLS AND EPIGRAMS.

IDYLLS AND EPIGRAMS.

I.

HOME the maid came from her lover's meeting,
Came with reddened hands.—The mother questioned:
"Wherewith have thy hands got reddened, Maiden?"
Said the maiden: "I have plucked some roses,
And upon the thorns my hands have wounded."
She again came from her lover's meeting,
Came with crimson lips.—The mother questioned:
"Wherewith have thy lips got crimson, Maiden?"
Said the maiden: "I have eaten strawberries,
And my lips I with their juice have painted."
She again came from her lover's meeting,
Came with pallid cheeks.—The mother questioned:
"Wherewith are thy cheeks so pallid, Maiden?"
Said the Maiden: "Make a grave, oh, Mother!
Hide me there, and place a cross thereover,

And cut on the cross what now I tell thee:—
Once she came home, and her hands were reddened,
For betwixt her lover's hands they reddened.
Once she came home, and her lips were crimson,
'Neath her lover's lips they had grown crimson.
Last, she came home, and her cheeks were pallid,
For they blanched beneath her lover's treason."

II.

FIRST asunder burst the brook's first bubbles,
    First depart the spring-time's first-blown flowers,
But thy first love, heart in youth rejoicing,
Will outlive a long time any other.

III.

OF his good luck spoke thus once a bridegroom:
    "Sunday next the last time banns are published,
Monday next I celebrate my wedding,
Thursday next my bride I bring home with me."
Sunday came—the last time banns were published,
Monday came—the wedding celebrated,
Thursday came—the house-warming was given,
But a house-warming in tears and sorrow,
For home to the grave his bride he carried.

IV.

FIFTEEN years the boy attained—believing
  Yet that no love in the world existed,
And he lived for five more years—believing,
Not e'en then, love in the world existed.
Came then suddenly a pretty maiden,
Who within a few short hours taught him,
What in twenty years he had not got at.

V.

MYRTLES twain there stand in Laura's window,
  And the one unceasingly she waters,
While the other in the pot is dried up;
Why is one thus tended, one forgotten?
From one and the same she did not get them.
But the one was from her youthful lover,
And the other from her husband—agèd.

VI.

WHEN the lovely May with wind-flowers cometh,
  Maids are wont to wreath their auburn tresses,
Hastening to the ring-dance round their May-pole,
While the dancing lasteth all are merry.

Merry she, who wears the pretty trinket,
Merry she, whose floweret-crown befits her,
Merry she, who feels her cheek grow ruddy;
Askest thou who of them all is merriest?
She who in the ring her bridegroom seeth.

VII.

O'ER the grave two poplar trees are rustling,
  Where a faithful youth in dust reposeth,
Planted erewhile by his maiden's hands there.
In the poplars' shade now grow the children
Which she bore unto another husband,
Chasing butterflies and culling flowers.

VIII.

MIDST some fresh-grown flowers through the greenwood
Walked the kindly maiden very lonely,
And she broke a new-born rose then saying,
Lovely flower, if thou but wings possessedst,
Would I send thee onward to my lover;
Two light messages I then would fasten,
On the right wing one, on the left the other.
One: that he should do no less than kiss thee,
And the other: Hither back should send thee.

IX.

IN her wooer's arms there wept a maiden,
    And bewailed her miserable fortune:
"Only yesternight, oh youth belovéd,
"Burnt my cottage, burnt my cattle also,
"All, ah, all, I in the world posseséd!"
In his soul the youth rejoiced then, thinking:
"Is the faithful maiden's cottage burnt up,
"Doubly will she henceforth love my cottage;
"Are he many herds of cattle burnt up,
"Doubly then my herds her heart will gladden;
"Has she lost all earthly goods, then shall I
"Be unto her doubly, doubly precious."

X.

IN the Park once built a pair of finches.
    In the spring the male sang without ceasing,
In the summer 'gan he to grow silent,
And by autumn grows he mute entirely.
Wherefore?—Why, so long as spring-time lasted
Thought he of his mate and of love only;
But with summer-tide came cares upon him,
For his home and for his tiny young ones;
And with autumn came the days on chilly,
And a longing only hence to fly off.

XI.

BUTTERFLIES, babes of spring,
　　Laughing wee flowerets, ye,
Bushes and verdant trees,
Wither, oh, wither soon;
Pictures of youth to me,
Pictures of love to me,
Wither, oh wither, soon!
Sold to an old man's breast,
I have no love for you.

XII.

"SPRINGTIME flieth swiftly,
　　Swifter still the summer;
Long the autumn tarries,
Longer still the winter;
Soon, oh, cheeks so beauteous,
Shall you have to wither,
Never more to blossom."
Then the youth made answer:
"Still in days of autumn
Springtime's memories cheer us;
Into days of winter
Reach the summer's harvests;

Spring is free to vanish,
Free the cheek to wither,
Let us only love now,
Let us only kiss now!"

XIII.

BENT 'gainst the fence the youth
    Stood at his maiden's arm,
Looked o'er a meadow mown:
"Summer's fair tide hath flown,
Flowers have all withered now;
Nathless thy cheek is fair,
Roses and lilies there
Bloom still as erst they did."
Spring came again, and then
Stood he there,—but alone:
Gone was the maiden—lay
Withered within earth's breast;
Green was the mead again,
Laughing with flowers o'erspread.

XIV.

MINNA sat the grove in,
    Looked upon the wreath
All of roses woven,
On her lap beneath.

And a tear she shed then
On the flowers below,
Prayed the gentle maid then
To the fair wreath so:
"Once thou hast surrounded
My youth's head, fair thing,
Breathe thou but around it
Balm of love and spring.
If thou may'st not stay there
On the yellow hair,
Then thou must betray there
Minna's hidden tear."

XV.

NATURE, ah, how could I ever
  Have offended thee?
Others gav'st thou beauty, never
  Beauty gav'st to me.
Oft outside the ring completed
  I am left behind,
To plain me, no look is meted,
  Not a friend I find.
Beats like others' hearts mine own, and
  Loves as well as they,—
Wherefore must I walk alone, and
  Be despised alway?

XVI.

COUNSELS three the mother gave her daughter:
  Not to sigh, and not be discontented,
And to kiss no young man whatsoever.—
Mother, if thy daughter trespass never,
Trespass never 'gainst your last-named counsel,
She will trespass 'gainst the first two, surely.

XVII.

ALL Saint John's Eve spends the maiden knitting
  Round the soft stems of the verdant corn-blades
Silken ribbons, all of various colours;
But she goes out, on the morning after,
To inquire into her fate in future.
Now then, hear, how there the maid behaveth:
Has the black stalk grown,—the stalk of sorrow,—
Talketh she and grieveth with the others.
Has the red stalk grown,—the stalk of gladness,—
Talks she and rejoiceth with the others.
Has the green stalk grown,—the stalk of love,—then
Keeps she silent, in her heart rejoicing.

XVIII.

To a fountain spake a youth right angry:
    Fountain, meadow's eye, thou naughty fountain,
Thousand times my maiden has already
Mirrored in thine azure lap her visage;
But thou guardest not the lovely image,
Thou preservest not my maiden's features.
When she goes, her image, too, is vanished,
And thereafter vainly search I for it.
Shall I punish thee, thou naughty fountain,
Stir thy billow muddy, dig thee out, and
Then tread down the flowery banks around thee?

Then the fountain prayed a prayer, saying:
"Youth, and why should I by thee be punished,
Why my billow muddied, why be dug out,
And down-trod the flowery banks around me?
I am but a daughter of the Water,
Have no blood, and have no fervid pulses,
Do not love, nor have I love returnèd.
Worse it is, that in thy very bosom,
In thine own heart's very fervid fountain
Seldom lasts the maiden's memory longer,
Than the while she stands in beauty for thee."

XIX.

TO her aged mother said the daughter:
   "Will my wedding not come off next autumn?"
Said the Mother: "Let it wait till springtime;
Spring, my daughter, suiteth best for marriage;
Even birds do build their nests in springtime."
"Why is spring the fittest time for marriage?
What of birds, that build their nests in springtime?
Every season, dearest mother, suiteth
Those who have but love for every season."

XX.

EDWARD spake thus to the Star of morning:
   "Dearest Morning-star, thou, heaven's daughter!
Say, what does Amanda, when she rises,
And the light veil throws across her shoulder?"
Answered him the Morning-star thus, saying:
"When, good youth, Amanda wakes and rises,
And the veil throws o'er her back, she goeth
To her window, looks on me, and weepeth,
And then turneth she her glances westward."
Edward spoke again, and this he uttered:
"Good, that she looks on the Star of morning,
This her purity of heart bespeaketh;

Good, that she should look upon it weeping,
This the softness of her heart bespeaketh.
Yet the best, that she should look to westward,
For to westward lieth Edward's bower."

XXI.

ONCE the boy said to his maiden:
"Off thou fleest, dearest maiden,
Every time I try to catch thee.
But now say, say, didst thou ever
Find secure and safe a shelter,
Till to my embrace thou fleddest?"

XXII.

TO a peasant's cottage came a warrior,
Bowed with years, a wooden leg to walk with.
Calm, for him the peasant filled a glass up,
Offering it, addressed the poor old soldier:
"Father, tell me, what did'st thou think of it,
"When in battle foemen did surround thee,
"Shots were cracking, and the bullets whistling?"
Raised his glass and answered the old soldier:
"Like thyself, when sometimes in the autumn
"Hail around thee whistles, lightning flashes,
"While thou'rt saving, for thine own, the harvest."

XXIII.

ONCE a youth stood at a maiden's window,
    Three long evenings after one another,
Knocked and prayed that he might yet be let in;
On the first he got but threats and scolding,
On the second got he words and prayers,
On the third he got the window open.

XXIV.

'NEATH the lake-shore pines a youth was playing
    By a bay of Saimen sung by minstrels.
From the billowy halls the Sprite then saw him,
Looked with love upon the youth's great beauty,
Wishing to allure him down unto him.
First an old man on the strand appeared he,
But the merry boy fled forth before him;
As a youth then on the strand appeared he,
But the merry youth no longer tarried;
Last, into a frisky foal transfigured,
Stepped he forth, and bounded mid'st the greenwood.
When the youth beheld the foal so frisky,
Went he gently, luringly, towards him,
Seized in haste his mane, and bounding mounted,
Longing now to have a ride right merry;

But into the deep, that very moment,
Fled the Sprite off with his charming booty.
To the strand came down the youth's own mother,
Searching for her child in tears and sorrow.
From the billowy halls the Sprite then saw her,
Looked with love upon the woman's beauty,
Wishing to allure her down unto him.
First an old man on the strand appeared he,
But the grieving woman fled before him,
As a youth then on the strand appeared he,
But the mourning woman would not tarry:
Last, into the merry youth transfigured,
Lay he glad and rocked upon the billow.
When the mother saw her son lamented,
Sprang she to his arms, into the billows,
Longing to redeem him from the peril.
But into the deep, that very moment,
Fled the Sprite off with his charming booty.

XXV.

HIGH 'mid Sarijärvis' moors resided
    Peasant Paavo on a frost-bound homestead,
And the soil with earnest arm was tilling;
But awaited from the Lord the increase.
And he dwelt there with his wife and children,

By his sweat his scant bread with them eating,
Digging ditches, ploughing up, and sowing.
Spring came on, the drift from cornfields melted,
And with it away flowed half the young blades;
Summer came, burst forth with hail the shower,
And with it the ears were half down beaten;
Autumn came, and frost took the remainder.
Paavo's wife then tore her hair, and spake thus:
"Paavo, old man, born to evil fortune,
Let us beg, for God hath us forsaken;
Hard is begging, but far worse is starving."
Paavo took the good-wife's hand, and spake thus:
"Nay, the Lord but trieth, not forsaketh,
Mix thou in the bread a half of bark now,
I shall dig out twice as many ditches,
And await then from the Lord the increase.
Half bark in the bread the good-wife mixed then,
Twice as many ditches dug the old man,
Sold the sheep, and bought some rye, and sowed it.
Spring came on, the drift from cornfields melted,
And with it away flowed half the young blades:
Summer came, burst forth with hail the shower,
And with it the ears were half down beaten,
Autumn came, and frost took the remainder.
Paavo's wife then smote her breast, and spake thus:
"Paavo, old man, born to evil fortune,

Let us perish, God hath us forsaken,
Hard is dying, but much worse is living."
Paavo took the good-wife's hand, and spake thus:
"Nay, the Lord but trieth, not forsaketh,
Mix thou in the bread of bark the double,
I will dig of double size the ditches,
But await then from the Lord the increase."
She mixed in the bread of bark the double,
He dug then of double size the ditches,
Sold the cows, and bought some rye and sowed it.
Spring came on, the drift from cornfields melted,
But with it away there flowed no young blades.
Summer came, burst forth with hail the shower,
But with it the ears were not down beaten,
Autumn came, and frost, the cornfields shunning,
Let them stand in gold to bide the reaper.
Then fell Paavo on his knee and spake thus:
"Aye, the Lord but trieth, not forsaketh."
And his mate fell on her knees, and spake thus:
"Aye, the Lord but trieth, not forsaketh."
But with gladness spoke she to the old man:
"Paavo, joyful to the scythe betake thee!
Now 'tis time for happy days and merry.
Now 'tis time to cast the bark away, and
Bake our bread henceforth of rye entirely."
Paavo took the good-wife's hand, and spake thus:

"Woman, he endureth trials only,
Who a needy neighbour ne'er forsaketh;
Mix thou in the bread a half of bark still,
For all frost-nipped stands our neighbour's cornfield."

XXVI.

FROM her mother had the girl a keepsake,
    Had a bracelet, set with pearls and diamonds,
One of value scarcely to be measured.
Then two wooers came and stood before her.
One of them was proud and rich and mighty,
But he wooed the maiden's bracelet only.
And the other, he was poor and modest,
But the maiden's heart he courted only.
Then the stepmother said to the daughter:
"Take the wealthy, and reject the poor one;
Fair is gold with poverty compared."
Vainly wept remonstrating the maiden.
But the day the banns were to be published,
In the mother's rooms was found no maiden,
At the stead, nor 'mid the park's stems either,
But upon the strand beside the ocean.
Thither came her mother and her wooer,
In a kind voice speaking to the maiden:
"Come with us to feasting and to gladness,
For to-day the banns are to be published."

But the maid drew from her belt the bracelet,
Took it in her own white hand then, saying,
See, who little has, is pleased with little;
He, who owneth much, still more doth covet.
Years innumerable has the ocean
Swallowed wealth, accumulated treasures,
Yet demandeth still my golden jewel.
So she said, and from the strand afar she
Threw her bracelet forth into the ocean.
Her the rich one left exasperated,
And the girl's stepmother cried in anger:
"Luckless one, what is it, thou art doing?
Never look thou more for any highness,
Never gold shall glitter in thy dwelling,
And no more beholdest thou thy bracelet."
But the noble maiden laughed and answered:
"What to future happiness is highness,
What to life with love is gold and glitter,
What to my youth's heart would be the bracelet?"

XXVII.

TAVASTLANDER large was Ojan Paavo,
    Large and mighty 'midst the sons of Finland,
Steady, as a rock o'ergrown with pine-trees,
Bold and quick and powerful, as a stormwind.
Fir-trees had he from the soil uprooted,

Smitten bears down with his arm's strength only,
Lifted horses over lofty fences,
And like straws had bent the boldest wrestlers.
And now stood the sturdy Ojan Paavo,
Proud and mighty at the law-court holding.
At the home-stead, 'mongst the folk he stood there,
Like a pine-tree towering o'er the brushwood:
And he raised his voice, and thus he challenged:
"Is there one of woman born and nurtured,
Who is able on this spot to hold me,
On this same spot only for a moment,
That one straight may take my wealthy homestead
That one win also my silver treasures,
That one own my many herds of cattle,
That one's own I'll be with soul and body!"
Thus unto the folk spoke Ojan Paavo.
But affrighted stood the village lads there,
Silent in the presence of the proud one;
And not one of them stepped out towards him.

And with wonder and with love were gazing
All the maidens on the stout young hero,
For he stood, the sturdy Ojan Paavo,
Like a pine-tree towering o'er the brushwood,
And his eye like heaven's star was flaming,
And his brow as clear as day was shining,
And his yellow hair fell o'er his shoulder,

As cascades fall sunlit down a mountain.

From the crowd of women out-stepped Anna,
She, the fairest of the village maidens,
Lovely, as a morning is to gaze at.
And she stepped out swift to Ojan Paavo,
Threw around his neck her arms so supple,
Placed her heart unto his heart quite closely,
And, his cheek against her own cheek pressing,
Bade him tear himself from her away then.
And the sturdy fellow stood there vanquished,
From the place he could not stir or struggle,
But said, giving in, unto the maiden:
"Anna, Anna! I have lost my wager.
Thou may'st straightway take my wealthy homestead,
Thou may'st win also my silver treasures,
Thou may'st own my many herds of cattle,
And thine own I am with soul and body."

XXVIII.

CAUGHT.

ON the ruddy river's bottom
    For some pearls a youth was fishing,
Found a pearl, as blue as heaven,
As the star of heaven rounded.
Lay within the pearl a maiden,
And she prayed a prayer, saying:

"Sacrifice thy pearl, oh, youth, now,
Break my prison, and release me;
In return a look all grateful
Will I give thee for my freedom!"

"No, by God, my darling maiden,
For the pearl is far too precious;
Bear but quietly thy fetter,
Many bore by far a worse one!"
Gently broke the crust the maiden;
Like the morning's glow in beauty
She beside the youth did shoot up.
Golden locks her forehead covered,
Rosy-hued her cheeks were glowing.—
Dumb, and captured by her beauty,
Stood the youth for three full hours;
When the third had struck, then prayed he
Silently a prayer, saying:
"Sacrifice thy beauty, maiden,
Break my prison, and release me;
In return a tear all grateful
Will I give thee for my freedom!"
"No, by God, oh, youth, my darling,
For the pearl is far too precious;
Bear but quietly thy fetter,
Many bore by far a worse one!"
M.

XXIX.

THE EARLY SORROW.

ROSES cull'dst thou for thy merry sister,
    Poppies kept'st thyself.
Rose betokens life and love, oh, maiden,
Poppy, cold and death.
Hast of heart's enjoyments no foreboding—
Or, pale angel, say,
Own'st thou at fifteen a fate already
To betoken thus?

XXX.

THE MAIDEN'S SEASONS.

WALKED the maid, one wintry morning,
    In the rime-besprinkled woodland,
Saw a withered rose, and spake thus:
"Grieve not, grieve not, poor wee floweret,
That thy fair time has flown over;
Thou hast lived, and known enjoyment,
Thou hast had thy spring and gladness,
Ere the winter's cold o'ertook thee.
Worse fate has my heart befallen:
It has spring at once and winter;
For a youth's eye is its spring-day
And my mother's is its winter."

XXXI.
LIKENESS.

HOW many waves dwell on the inlet,
How many thoughts within my bosom?
They seem to fly—and yet they tarry,
They seem to die—again revive though.
So different, yet so like each other,
So many, and yet all the self-same!—
On self-same sea, by self-same breezes
They all are stirred up,
From self-same breast they all are stirred up
By love the self-same.

XXXII.
THE BIRD.

OPEN is my maiden's window,
If I were a bird unknown, I
Would at once fly in unto her.
In a cage then she would place me,
She would fill the glass with water,
She would fill with seed the drawer.
But then I should thus address her:
Girl, away with seed and water;
Know, that this thy bird so merry,
Drinketh only tender tears, and
Lives but on caress and kisses.

XXXIII.

THE FIRST KISS.

BY silver-clouds' edge evening's star was seated,
From dusky grove her thus a maiden greeted:
"Say, star of evening, what is thought in Heaven,
"When first a kiss is to a lover given?"
And heaven's daughter coy was heard replying:
"The angel hosts of light, the Earth then eying,
Their own bliss see reflected there;—Death keepeth
Alone his eye then turned away—and weepeth."

XXXIV.

FLY AWAY NOT.

WOULD'ST thou know, thou roguish maiden,
How they catch the thrush in autumn?
I will be myself the fowler,
Thou pretend to be the throstle.
Mark now how the fowler speaketh:
"Fly not off, thou pretty throstle;
Sit thou still amidst the berries,
For the snare no harm will do thee,
For the snare will but caress thee."
Ah, thou rogue, thou'st let me catch thee,
Kiss me, and I'll let thee go then.

XXXV.
THE KISS'S HOPE.

WHILE I sat in dreams beside a fountain,
    Heard I how a kiss, my lips frequenting,
Softly uttered this unto another:
"See, she comes there, see the modest maiden
Comes already; and in a few hours
On her rosy lips I shall be sitting;
Faithfully the whole day she will bear me.
Care not e'en to taste a single strawberry,
Lest I with the juice of it be blended;
Care not e'en to drink of the clear fountain,
Lest against the glass' brim I be crushéd;
Care not e'en of love one word to whisper,
Lest she breathe me off her lips of roses."

XXXVI.
LOVE.

ONCE a dame this wise reviled her daughter:
    "Girl, against Love I have often warned thee,
And I find my warnings go for nothing."
Said the daughter: "Be not angry, mother:
Though the door I bolted to escape him,
With each mote he'd fly into the chamber.

If abroad I went but to eschew him;
Should I hear in every breeze his sighing,
If I shut my eyes and ears together,
Like a rogue my heart he then would enter."

XXXVII.
THE DIFFERENCE.

How I sat with head on hand dejected,
    From the sill a sparrow gay detected,
Lightly pecked upon the pane and said,
" Boy, why griev'st thou there? Be comforted!
With a seed, spring in the fields displayeth,
Drop of rain, that from the snowdrift strayeth,
With my bride a love-note to afford,
Am I rich, blessed, happy as the Lord."—
Say, poor sparrow, are wings to me given,
Like thyself, to fly from earth to heaven?
Have I voice, like thee, for love? beside,
And the worst of all,—have I a bride?

XXXVIII.
THE DREAM.

On the bed I laid me down aweary,
    To forget in sleep regret and sorrow;
But a dream stole softly to my pillow,
And into my ear it thus did whisper:

Wake, for she is here the lovely maiden,
Look up that thou mayst receive her kisses.
And my eye I cast up then with gladness.
Where's the dream? It like to smoke has vanished:
Where's the maid? far off o'er land and water:
Where's the kiss? Ah, only in my longing!

XXXIX.
THE DISREGARDED ONE.

EAR by ear rocks in the wheat-field,
    Grain by grain in the ear is hiding,
So, each fleeting word thou utteredst,
Waxeth in my faithful bosom.
Cruel youth, and most ungrateful!
Tillers go to save their harvests,
Thou dost only sow, and leavest
To the birds of air the reaping,
To the snows and to the wind-blasts.

XL.
THE FLOWER-DEALER.

FOUR years old the boy was sitting
    On the strand beside his sister,
Cut of bark a ship with rigging,
Freighted then the ship with flowers,

Hired a crew of ants to man it,
And said to the ants' commander:
"Put to sea now, dauntless sailor;
Sail off then; return anon and
Sell on yonder strand my cargo,
Some for gold, and some for pearls, and
Some for other pretty playthings."
Stroked his yellow locks the sister,
Drew a sigh, and spoke as follows:
"Child of four years old, thou sellest
Flowers that harmless grace the seaboard,
When to twenty-four thou reachest,
Thou wilt barter faithful bosoms,
Some for gold, and some for pearls, and
Some for other pretty playthings."

XLI.

GRIEF AND JOY.

GRIEF and joy together
    In my heart abided,
Grief within one chamber,
Joy within the other,
Both unreconciléd.
Now the one bore sway there,
Now the other wholly.

Since the one love came there,
She the door has opened,
And the twain appeaséd.
For my grief is bliss now,
And my joy is sadness.

XLII.

BUTTERFLY POST.

AT the opened arbour window
   Sat one summer morn a maiden;
But from flowers in fields surrounding
Came a butterfly goldwingéd,
Sat upon the maiden's tresses.
Shut she straight the window; caught and
Tried to tame the butterfly then.
"Fly not forth, thou pretty prisoner,
Feast on kisses, take caresses,
On the hand remain thou quiet!"
Vainly! each time she released him,
Flew he fluttering 'gainst the window;
Touched at length by his disquiet,
Oped the pretty maid the window:
"Fly thou forth, ungrateful, fly thou,
To thy like bear thou this message:
Bid them not to care to come here,
When they never care to tarry."

XLIII.
TROUBLE NOT THE MAIDEN'S SOUL.

BY the brook the maiden sat,
   And within it washed her feet,
Sang a bird above her thus:
"Trouble not the brooklet, maid,
No more see I there the sky."
Turned the maiden up her eye,
And with tearful look she spoke:
"Grieve not for the brooklet, thou,
That will soon be clear again.
Once when thou beheldest me
Standing here beside a youth,
Sooth, thou should'st have said to him:
"Trouble not the maiden's soul,
It will ne'er be clear again,
Ne'er reflect the heaven more."

XLIV.
THE SUMMER NIGHT.

ON the still lake's waters carried,
   All one summer night I tarried,
Thoughtless to the billows' crew there
From the boat my line I threw there.
On the shore a thrush was chanting,
Till for breath he nigh was panting;

And I spoke thus half offended:
"Better that thy beak were bended
Underneath thy wing, for glaring
Day thy notes and sallies sparing."
And I heard him bold replying:
"Let alone the rod thou'rt plying,
Saw'st thou high o'er land and mere too,
Thou would'st sing all night long here, too."
And I lifted up mine eye then,
Light was earth and light the sky then.
Sky and strand and wave displayed, and
Brought into my mind my maid, and
As the woodland bird had said, I
Sang the self-same song already.

XLV.

PEACE.

OFT my mother says, at leisure:
 "Child, thou hast a twofold treasure;
Both for evil times reserve thou,
Peace and Innocence preserve thou!"
"Mother, peace is past and over,
Shall I ever that recover?
Bid me not forget him ever,
Who has taken and keeps it—never,
Never, till we both are mated,
Can my peace be reinstated."

XLVI.

ALTERED.

FORMERLY all day long I was twitted,
  Bodice now, and collar now, misfitted,
Now my hair was done up too untidy,
Never long enough my mirror eyed I.
Now is all this altered! "Say, whatever
Ails thee, girl, that thou art ready never?
How thou dost bedeck thee—'tis amazing!
Hast not done yet at the mirror gazing?"
Has some witchcraft in my mind then caught me?
Who can such a change as this have wrought me?
None, my heart is silently declaring,
Save the youth, p'rhaps, and the ring I'm wearing.

XLVII.

THE LONG DAY.

ERST, when my love was here,
  Spring-day was short to me.
Now he is gone away
An autumn day is long.
"Ah, how the day does fly!"
So say the others now.
I: "Oh, how slow it is!

Oh, would it only fly!
Cometh not evening soon?
Cometh not night-time's rest?"

XLVIII.
CHARMS.

I LOOK on the bevy of maidens,
  I gaze and I gaze on for ever;
The fairest I'd like to make choice of,
Yet falter for ever in choosing.
The one has the eyes that are brightest,
The other the cheeks that are freshest,
The third has the lips that are fullest,
The fourth has the heart that is warmest.—
I cannot find one but she lacketh
A something to capture my fancy,
Not one of them can I throw over!
Oh, could I but kiss all together!

XLIX.
AMOR.

HE my heart hath never wounded,
  Never, as dead volumes teach us,
Stole he forth with bow and arrows,
Innocence was all his cunning,

Beauty was his only weapon.
"Lovely boy, wouldst thou but come now,
For my heart is warm and open."
He obeyed, at once, and since then
Just as he is fond of staying,
I myself am fain to own him.

L.

THE COMPLIANT ONE.

IN the field, as golden sheaves I tied up,
   Stood beside me there the youthful Adolf,
In his hand he held the scythe, his gun was
Leaning 'gainst a stump upon the border;
But within the marsh that lay below it,
Near the strand, a teal cried in the rushes.

To the gun then sprang the brave young sportsman;
But his arm I seized, at once, and prayed him:
"Let alone the poor teal, do, my Adolf!
Leave her undisturbed, if but for my sake."
Instantly his gun he put aside then,
And took to his scythe as glad as ever.

But within my mind I often ponder:
Strange indeed is he, the handsome Adolf;
For a friendly word from my lips falling,
Leaves he what his heart doth most delight in;

If my eyes throw hearty glances at him
He does gladly what he once avoided,
For a friendly kiss and fond embraces,
I believe, he'd go through fire and water.

LI.

THE SINGLE HOUR.

Alone I bided,
   He came alone too.
Across my pathway
His path was leading;
He did not tarry,
Yet thought to tarry,
Himself he spoke not,
And yet his eye spoke.—
Oh, thou unknown one,
Oh thou well-known one!
A day doth vanish,
A year o'erpasseth,
One memory ever
The other chaseth,
That briefest hour
Stays with me ever,
That bitterest hour,
That sweetest hour.

LII.

THE THORN.

THORN, oh, sapling of my kindred,
　　Wrapped in winter's ice thou'rt scornéd,
Clothed in spines art hated too.
But I think, when spring-time cometh,
Burst'st thou forth in leaves and roses,
And no plant on earth existeth
Sweet and lovely like to thee.

Oh, how many a thorn-stem is there
Standing naked out in Nature,
Which requireth love alone,
　ut a sun-glance of a heart, to
Clothe and deck itself in roses,
And each being's joy to be!

LIII.

THREE AND THREE.

FROM the lofty tower were looking
　　Three young girls out o'er the ocean,
Saw three ships in sail approaching,
And thus spoke the eldest sister:
"Sisters, look, our father's ships are
Coming back from distant countries;

Here we are three sisters waiting,
Three commanders steer the vessels;
"He who first is safe in harbour,
He shall have my wreath of roses,
If therewith he be contented."
And the second sister speaketh:
"Him, who next shall make the harbour,
Give I my bouquet of flowers,
If therewith he be contented."
Then the youngest sister speaketh:
"He, who maketh last the harbour,
Shall receive my glad embraces
If he be the brave Augustus."

LIV.

THE NORTH.

LEAVES they are falling,
Lakes they are freezing,—
Swans that are flitting,
Sail ye, oh, sail ye,
Sadly to southward,
Seeking a make-shift,
Longing back hither;

Plough ye its lakes then,
Our lakes regretting.
Then shall an eye be-
hold you from palm-trees'
shadow, and say thus:
"Languishing Swans, oh,
What a strange magic
Lingers o'er Northland?
He, who from southward
Longeth, his longing
Seeketh a heaven."

LV.

THE RARE BIRD.

AS, at eve, he in the chamber entered,
Thus her son the aged mother scolded:
"Son, unto thy snares each day thou goest,
And each day returnest empty-handed,
Thou art either heedless, or art foolish,
Since while others catch, thou catchest nothing."

Eagerly the youth returned this answer:
"What of that, though fortune be unequal,
We are not all for the same birds fowling.
There, beyond the moor, by yon small cottage,

Is a rare bird, dearest Mother, dwelling;
I have stalked it all throughout the autumn,
Now, in winter, I at length have caught it,
But when Spring comes I shall bring it hither.
Strange that bird is, yonder, it is wingless,
Has instead embracing arms and bosom;
Has no down, but silk-like flowing tresses;
Has no bill, but two lips sweetly rounded."

LVI.

WILT EXCHANGE OUR FORTUNES?

"GROWN up on the bank, there
    Of the brook, that swelleth,
Washed by every eddy,
What a life unquiet,
Art thou leading, flower!"
Thus the flower answered:
"If the torrent spare me,
If the torrent vex me,
Yet all my disquiet
Lasts one fleeting summer.
Wilt exchange our fortunes,
Maid, washed by the torrent
In a lover's bosom?"

LVII.

HER MESSAGE.

COME, thou sorrowing north-wind!
　　Every time thou comest,
Bear from her a message.
Comest thou in breezes,
Bear thou forth her sighing,
Comest thou in blusters,
Bear thou her complaining;
Comest thou in storm-winds,
Bear thou forth her woe-shrieks.
"Woe to me, the perjured,
Woe to me, forlorn one!
From the old man's arms and
From his chilly kisses,
Who will once more bring me
To my youth, the warm one,
Back unto my first love?"

LVIII.

THE WIND-FLOWER.

WIND-FLOWER, spring-time's first-born blossom,
　　If I culled thee, if I gave thee,
To the loved one, to the cold one!—
Did I cull thee, I should give thee,

Did I give thee, I should say then:
"Near the snowdrift's edge, oh maiden,
Waxed the spring-time's first-born blossom,
As beside thy heart's ice buddeth
Into bloom my love devoted,
Trembling at the wintry chill, but
Quelled not by it; neither shorn off."

LIX.

MEETING.

SAT a maid one summer's evening,
   Viewed her face within the fountain:
"Oh, good Heavens, I am pretty!
But what booteth me my beauty,
Since the youth I am in love with
Does not see me, does not hear me?
Rose, that now beside me glowest,
Take away my lips' hue ruddy!
Crimson-sprinkled cloud in heaven,
Take away my cheeks' hue crimson!
Pallid star beyond the cloud-haze,
Take away my eyes' fresh brightness;
Last, oh, grave, take the remainder!"
This the youth with roguish pleasure
From the nearest bush had caught up,

And he springeth forth towards her,
Just the sought one, just the found one.
But forthwith her lips he kisses:
"Took the rose the lips' hue ruddy!"
And he laid his cheek 'gainst her cheek:
"Took the cloud the cheeks' hue crimson!"
And into her eye he gazéd:
"Took the star the eyes' fresh brightness!"
And his arms he flung around her:
"Took the grave now the remainder;"
For it is the grave, oh, maiden,
Wherefrom no one e'er escapeth!

LX.

LAUGHTER.

LAUGHTER had got no home,
　　Down-cast it roamed about,
Came to the high one's mouth:
"Can I find lodging here?"—
"Pride dwells already here."

Laughter had got no home,
Down-cast it roamed about,
Came to the scholar's mouth:
"Can I find lodging here?"—
"Earnest dwells here before."

Laughter had got no home,
Down-cast it roamed about,
Came to my maiden's mouth:
"Can I find lodging here?"—
"Love dwells already here,
Just now the kiss arrived,
Thou'rt just the one we missed."

LXI.

THE TEARS.

WHEN o'er the wood the sun had risen already,
    And o'er the dale's dew shed his glow, the maiden
With looks of tearful joy received her lover.
He looked into her eye, and laughed, and spake thus:
"Last night in tears I left thee, now I come back,
I find thee weeping also, darling maiden!
Tell me, what difference 'twixt these tears existeth.
"The selfsame difference," softly said the maiden,
"As 'twixt the dew of eve and dew of morning.
The one the sun lights up and dissipateth,
The other dreary all night long remaineth."

LXII.

EROS' CHANGE.

"EROS, naughty fellow," so said Pallas,
"For thy lust of wounding every bosom
Should'st thou to a beast of prey be changéd,
To a kite with wings and crooked talons,
All in vain the host of birds pursuing."
Eros laughed, and only said: "Well, try it!
Since thou to a kite hast Amor changéd,
Every bird will now be torn to pieces."

THE END.

www.ingramcontent.com/pod-product-compliance
Lightning Source LLC
Chambersburg PA
CBHW032143230426
43672CB00011B/2437